Ogre 3D 1.7

Beginner's Guide

Create real-time 3D applications using Ogre 3D
from scratch

Felix Kerger

BIRMINGHAM - MUMBAI

Ogre 3D 1.7
Beginner's Guide

First published: November 2010

Production Reference: 1191110

Published by Packt Publishing Ltd.
32 Lincoln Road
Olton
Birmingham, B27 6PA, UK.

ISBN: 978-1-849512-48-0

www.packtpub.com

Cover Image by John M. Quick (john.m.quick@gmail.com)

Credits

Author
Felix Kerger

Reviewers
Manuel Bua

Gregory Junker

Acquisition Editor
Usha Iyer

Development Editors
Hyacintha D'Souza

Mayuri Kokate

Technical Editor
Prashant Macha

Copy Editor
Leonard D'Silva

Indexers
Hemangini Bari

Monica Ajmera Mehta

Editorial Team Leader
Mithun Sehgal

Project Team Leader
Ashwin Shetty

Project Coordinator
Poorvi Nair

Proofreader
Sandra Hopper

Graphics
Nilesh Mohite

Production Coordinator
Adline Swetha Jesuthas

Cover Work
Adline Swetha Jesuthas

About the Author

Felix Kerger is a Computer Science student at the Technical University of Darmstadt and has been developing 3D real-time applications using Ogre 3D for more than five years. He has given several talks on software development and 3D real-time applications at different conferences and has been working for three years as an assistant researcher at the Fraunhofer Institute for Computer Graphics Research. He also works as a freelance journalist and reports yearly from the Game Developer Conference Europe.

I would like to thank the following persons, without whom this book wouldn't have been possible: Steve Streeting for devoting so much time to Ogre 3D and creating one of the best pieces of software I have had the pleasure to work with; my former teachers Ms. Oppel and Ms. Michel, who helped me write a report on which this book's idea is based ; my parents, who were a constant source of inspiration and motivation; Gregory Junker and Manuel Bua, my technical reviewers—their comments helped me no end and improved this book a lot; and, of course, the team at Packt for their constant help and advice.

About the Reviewers

Manuel Bua is a software and solutions architect from Trento, Italy. He has over 17 years' experience and has been involved in many small and large-scale software projects, at both the design and implementation levels.

His background and experience range from software development to reverse engineering, embracing both the desktop and the mobile platform; multithreading, parallel, and massively-parallel computing architectures also pique his interest greatly, as well as computational photography and games development.

In 2007, he joined Jooce's Research and Development division in Paris, France, holding the position of Chief Architect, engineering and optimizing their in-house, Actionscript-based virtual desktop platform connecting millions of people worldwide; during his staying, he also designed and implemented the compositing window manager governing windows transitions and effects, such as the well-known "Wobbly Windows," first introduced by Compiz on the (rocking!) Linux desktop.

He loves open standards and the open source culture. His desire to learn and to share his knowledge has led him to contribute to various projects, such as Ogre itself; he designed and programmed the original out-of-core implementation of what is known today as the "Compositor Framework," providing both the initial insight and the high-level concepts, laying the foundations for further research, work, and improvements.

He is currently employed at F4F Creative Factory, a design-inspired web and advertising agency based in Arco, Trento, in the roles of solutions architect, software engineer, and systems administrator.

Gregory Junker is the author of the APress book "Pro Ogre 3D Programming."

Table of Contents

Preface   1

Chapter 1: Installing Ogre 3D   7
Downloading and installing Ogre 3D   7
Time for action – downloading and installing Ogre 3D   7
Different versions of the Ogre 3D SDK   8
Exploring the SDK   9
The Ogre 3D samples   10
Time for action – building the Ogre 3D samples   11
The first application with Ogre 3D   12
Time for action – starting the project and configuring the IDE   12
ExampleApplication   15
Loading the first model   16
Time for action – loading a model   16
Summary   17

Chapter 2: The Ogre Scene Graph   19
Creating a scene node   19
Time for action – creating a scene node with Ogre 3D   19
How to work with the RootSceneNode   20
3D space   21
Scene graph   23
Setting the position of a scene node   24
Time for action – setting the position of a scene node   25
Rotating a scene node   26
Time for action – rotating a scene node   26
Scaling a scene node   29
Time for action – scaling a scene node   29
Using a scene graph the clever way   32
Time for action – building a tree using scene nodes   32

Have a go hero – adding a following ninja	**35**
Different spaces in a scene	**35**
Time for action – translating in World space	**36**
Different spaces in a 3D scene	38
Translating in local space	**40**
Time for action – translating in local and parent space	**40**
Rotating in different spaces	**42**
Time for action – rotating in different spaces	**42**
Scaling in different spaces	**45**
Summary	**45**
Chapter 3: Camera, Light, and Shadow	**47**
Creating a plane	**47**
Time for action – creating a plane	**47**
Representing models in 3D	50
Adding a point light	**51**
Time for action – adding a point light	**51**
Adding a spotlight	**53**
Time for action – creating a spotlight	**53**
Spotlights	55
Directional lights	**57**
Time for action – creating a directional light	**58**
The missing thing	**59**
Time for action – finding out what's missing	**59**
Adding shadows	**60**
Time for action – adding shadows	**60**
Creating a camera	**61**
Time for action – creating a camera	**61**
Creating a viewport	**64**
Time for action – doing something that illustrates the thing "in action"	**64**
Summary	**66**
Chapter 4: Getting User Input and Using the Frame Listener	**67**
Preparing a scene	**67**
Time for action – preparing a scene	**68**
Adding movement to the scene	**70**
Time for action – adding movement to the scene	**70**
FrameListener	72
Modifying the code to be time based rather than frame based	**73**
Time for action – adding time-based movement	**73**
Adding input support	**74**

Time for action – adding input support	**75**
Window handle	76
Adding movement to the model	**77**
Time for action – controlling Sinbad	**77**
Adding a camera	**79**
Time for action – making the camera work again	**79**
Mouse state	81
Adding wireframe and point render mode	**82**
Time for action – adding wireframe and point render mode	**82**
Adding a timer	**84**
Time for action – adding a timer	**84**
Summary	**85**

Chapter 5: Animating models with Ogre 3D	**87**
Adding animations	**87**
Time for action – adding animations	**88**
Playing two animations at the same time	**91**
Time for action – adding a second animation	**91**
Let's walk a bit	**93**
Time for action – combining user control and animation	**94**
Adding swords	**97**
Time for action – adding swords	**97**
Animations	99
Printing all the animations a model has	**100**
Time for action – printing all animations	**100**
Summary	**102**

Chapter 6: Scene Managers	**103**
Starting with a blank sheet	**103**
Time for action – creating a blank sheet	**104**
Getting the scene manager's type	**105**
Time for action – printing the scene manager's type	**105**
What does a scene manger do?	105
Octree	106
Another scene manager type	**108**
Time for action – using another scene manager	**108**
ResourceManager	109
setWorldGeometry	110
Creating our own model	**110**
Time for action – creating a model for displaying blades of grass	**110**
Manual object	113
Texture mapping	115

Adding volume to the blades of grass	116
Time for action – using more triangles for volume	116
Creating a field of grass	118
Time for action – building a field of grass	119
Exploring the name scheme	120
Time for action – printing the names	120
Static geometry	122
Time for action – using static geometry	122
Rendering pipeline	125
Indices	126
Summary	127

Chapter 7: Materials with Ogre 3D | 129

Creating a white quad	129
Time for action – creating the quad	130
Creating our own material	131
Time for action – creating a material	131
Materials	133
Texture coordinates take two	133
Time for action – preparing our quad	133
Using the wrapping mode with another texture	135
Time for action – adding a rock texture	135
Using another texture mode	137
Time for action – adding a rock texture	137
Using the mirror mode	138
Time for action – using the mirror mode	139
Using the border mode	140
Time for action – using the border mode	140
Changing the border color	141
Time for action – changing the border color	141
Scrolling a texture	143
Time for action – preparing to scroll a texture	143
Time for action – scrolling a texture	144
Animated scrolling	146
Time for action – adding animated scrolling	146
Inheriting materials	146
Time for action – inheriting from a material	147
Fixed Function Pipeline and shaders	149
Render Pipeline	150
Time for action – our first shader application	151
Writing a shader	155

Texturing with shaders	156
Time for action – using textures in shaders	156
What happens in the render pipeline?	158
Interpolating color values	159
Time for action – using colors to see interpolation	159
Replacing the quad with a model	160
Time for action – replacing the quad with a model	161
Making the model pulse on the x-axis	162
Time for action – adding a pulse	162
Summary	164
Chapter 8: The Compositor Framework	**165**
Preparing a scene	165
Time for action – preparing the scene	166
Adding the first compositor	167
Time for action – adding a compositor	167
How the compositor works	169
Modifying the texture	170
Time for action – modifying the texture	170
Inverting the image	172
Time for action – inverting the image	172
Combining compositors	173
Time for action – combining two compositor effects	173
Decreasing the texture count	175
Time for action – decreasing the texture count	175
Combining compositors in code	177
Time for action – combing two compositors in code	177
Something more complex	178
Time for action – complex compositor	178
Changing the number of pixels	182
Time for action – putting the number of pixels in the material	183
Setting the variable in code	185
Time for action – setting the variable from the application	185
Changing the number of pixels while running the application	188
Time for action – modifying the number of pixels with user input	188
Adding a split screen	193
Time for action – adding a split screen	194
Putting it all together	197
Time for action – selecting a color channel	198
Summary	203

Chapter 9: The Ogre 3D Startup Sequence   205

Starting Ogre 3D   205
Time for action – starting Ogre 3D   206
Adding resources   208
Time for action – loading the Sinbad mesh   208
Using resources.cfg   209
Time for action – using resources.cfg to load our models   209
   Structure of a configuration file   211
Creating an application class   211
Time for action – creating a class   212
Adding a FrameListener   215
Time for action – adding a FrameListener   215
Investigating the FrameListener functionality   216
Time for action – experimenting with the FrameListener implementation   216
Time for action – returning true in the frameStarted function   217
   Double buffering   218
Time for action – returning true in the frameRenderingQueued function   218
Time for action – returning true in the frameEnded function   219
Adding input   220
Time for action – adding input   220
Our own main loop   222
Time for action – using our own rendering loop   222
Adding a camera (again)   224
Time for action – adding a frame listener   224
Adding compositors   226
Time for action – adding compositors   226
Adding a plane   229
Time for action – adding a plane and a light   230
Adding user control   231
Time for action – controlling the model with the arrow keys   231
Adding animation   233
Time for action – adding animation   234
Summary   236

Chapter 10: Particle Systems and Extending Ogre 3D   239

Adding a particle system   239
Time for action – adding a particle system   240
  What is a particle system?   241
Creating a simple particle system   241
Time for action – creating a particle system   242
Some more parameters   244

Time for action – some new parameters	244
Other parameters	246
Time for action – time to live and color range	246
Turning it on and off again	247
Time for action – adding intervals to a particle system	247
Adding affectors	248
Time for action – adding a scaler affector	248
Changing colors	250
Time for action – changing the color	250
Two-way changing	253
Time for action – change depending on the lifetime of a particle	253
Even more complex color manipulations	255
Time for action – using complex color manipulation	255
Adding randomness	257
Time for action – adding randomness	257
Deflector	259
Time for action – using the deflector plane	259
Other emitter types	261
Time for action – using a box emitter	261
Emitting with a ring	262
Time for action – using a ring to emit particles	262
At the end, we would like some fireworks	264
Time for action – adding fireworks	264
Extending Ogre 3D	266
Speedtree	267
Hydrax	267
Caelum	267
Particle Universe	267
GUIs	267
CEGUI	267
BetaGUI	268
QuickGUI	268
Berkelium	268
Summary	268
The end	268
Appendix: Pop Quiz Answers	**269**
Chapter 1	269
Installing Ogre 3D	269
Chapter 2	270
Setting up the Environment	270

Chapter 3	**270**
Felix Gogo	270
Chapter 4	**271**
Felix Gogo	271
Chapter 5	**271**
The Book Inventory Bundle	271
Chapter 7	**272**
The Bookshelf: First Stab	**272**
Chapter 9	**272**
The Ogre 3D Startup Sequence	272
Chapter 10	**273**
How About a Graphical Interface?	273
Index	**275**

Preface

Creating 3D scenes and worlds is an interesting and challenging problem, but the results are hugely rewarding and the process to get there can be a lot of fun. This book is going to show you how you can create your own scenes and worlds with the help of Ogre 3D. Ogre 3D is one of the biggest open source 3D render engines and enables its users to create and interact freely with their scenes.

This book can't show all the details about Ogre 3D but rather provide a solid introduction with which you, as a reader, can start using Ogre 3D by yourself. After finishing the book, you will be able to use the documentation and the wiki to look up for the needed information and complex techniques, which aren't covered in this book.

What this book covers

Chapter 1, *Installing Ogre 3D*, shows how to get and configure Ogre 3D. We also create our first scene and start learning the internals of Ogre 3D

Chapter 2, *The Ogre Scene Graph*, introduces us to the concept of a scene graph and how it is used for describing 3D scenes

Chapter 3, *Camera, Light, and Shadow*, adds lights and shadows to our scene and also experiments with different camera settings

Chapter 4, *Getting User Input and using the Frame Listener*, adds interactivity to our application using user input

Chapter 5, *Animating Models with Ogre 3D*, will enhance our scene using animations to add more interactivity and realism

Chapter 6, *Scene Managers*, will introduce us to different concepts for organizing 3D scenes and what implication these choices will have

Chapter 7, Materials with Ogre 3D, will show us how to add a new level of detail and flexibility to our application using materials and shaders.

Chapter 8, The Compositor Framework, will show us how to add post processing effects to change the look of our complete scene with the knowledge about materials

Chapter 9, The Ogre 3D Startup Sequence, shows us how we can use Ogre 3D without the help of an `ExampleApplication` we had used previously

Chapter 10, Particle Systems and Extending Ogre 3D, gives an introduction to some more advanced techniques and perspectives that can be done with Ogre 3D

What you need for this book

You need a solid understanding of C++ and how to create applications using C++ for this book. Of course, you need a compiler to compile the example applications. This book uses Visual Studio as a reference, but any other compiler will also do. Your computer should have a graphic card with 3D capabilities. It would be best if the graphic card supports DirectX 9.0 because Ogre 3D is an open source software and we will download it in *Chapter 1*. So there is no need for you to have Ogre 3D already installed on your computer.

Who this book is for

If you ever wanted to develop 3D application with Ogre 3D, this example-driven book will enable you to do so. Understanding of C++ is needed to follow the examples in the book.

This book is an example-driven introduction to Ogre 3D. Each example shows some new features and you learn step-by-step to create complex scenes with different effects using Ogre 3D. After several examples discussing one topic, there is a do-it-yourself part where you will be challenged to solve problems on your own.

Conventions

In this book, you will find a number of styles of text that distinguish between different kinds of information. Here are some examples of these styles, and an explanation of their meaning.

Code words in text are shown as follows: "Delete all the old code in `createScene()`, except for the plane-related code."

A block of code is set as follows:

```
void MyFragmentShader2(float2 uv      : TEXCOORD0,
            out float4 color : COLOR,
            uniform sampler2D texture)
```

New terms and **important words** are shown in bold. Words that you see on the screen, in menus or dialog boxes for example, appear in the text like this: "Press **Ok** and start the Application. "

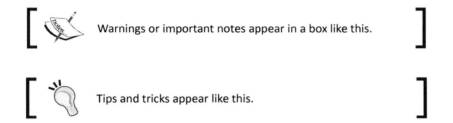

Warnings or important notes appear in a box like this.

Tips and tricks appear like this.

Reader feedback

Feedback from our readers is always welcome. Let us know what you think about this book—what you liked or may have disliked. Reader feedback is important for us to develop titles that you really get the most out of.

To send us general feedback, simply send an e-mail to feedback@packtpub.com, and mention the book title via the subject of your message.

If there is a book that you need and would like to see us publish, please send us a note in the **SUGGEST A TITLE** form on www.packtpub.com or e-mail suggest@packtpub.com.

If there is a topic that you have expertise in and you are interested in either writing or contributing to a book, see our author guide on www.packtpub.com/authors.

Customer support

Now that you are the proud owner of a Packt book, we have a number of things to help you to get the most from your purchase.

Downloading the example code for this book

You can download the example code files for all Packt books you have purchased from your account at `http://www.PacktPub.com`. If you purchased this book elsewhere, you can visit `http://www.PacktPub.com/support` and register to have the files e-mailed directly to you.

Downloading the color images of this book

We also provide you a PDF file that has color images of the screenshots used in this book. The color images will help you better understand the changes in the output. You can download this file from `https://www.packtpub.com/sites/default/files/2480_Ogre3D 1.7Beginner's Guide.`

Errata

Although we have taken every care to ensure the accuracy of our content, mistakes do happen. If you find a mistake in one of our books—maybe a mistake in the text or the code—we would be grateful if you would report this to us. By doing so, you can save other readers from frustration and help us improve subsequent versions of this book. If you find any errata, please report them by visiting `http://www.packtpub.com/support`, selecting your book, clicking on the **errata submission form** link, and entering the details of your errata. Once your errata are verified, your submission will be accepted and the errata will be uploaded on our website, or added to any list of existing errata, under the Errata section of that title. Any existing errata can be viewed by selecting your title from `http://www.packtpub.com/support`.

Piracy

Piracy of copyright material on the Internet is an ongoing problem across all media. At Packt, we take the protection of our copyright and licenses very seriously. If you come across any illegal copies of our works, in any form, on the Internet, please provide us with the location address or website name immediately so that we can pursue a remedy.

Please contact us at copyright@packtpub.com with a link to the suspected pirated material.

We appreciate your help in protecting our authors, and our ability to bring you valuable content.

Questions

You can contact us at questions@packtpub.com if you are having a problem with any aspect of the book, and we will do our best to address it.

1
Installing Ogre 3D

Downloading and installing a new library are the first steps of learning about and using it.

In this chapter, we shall do the following:

- ◆ Download and install Ogre 3D
- ◆ Have our development environment working with Ogre 3D
- ◆ Create our first scene rendered by Ogre 3D

So let's get on with it.

Downloading and installing Ogre 3D

The first step we need to take is to install and configure Ogre 3D.

Time for action – downloading and installing Ogre 3D

We are going to download the Ogre 3D SDK and install it so that we can work with it later.

1. Go to `http://www.ogre3d.org/download/sdk`.

2. Download the appropriate package. If you need help picking the right package, take a look at the next *What just happened* section.

3. Copy the installer to a directory you would like your OgreSDK to be placed in.

4. Double-click on the Installer; this will start a self extractor.

5. You should now have a new folder in your directory with a name similar to **OgreSDK_vc9_v1-7-1**.

6. Open this folder. It should look similar to the following screenshot:

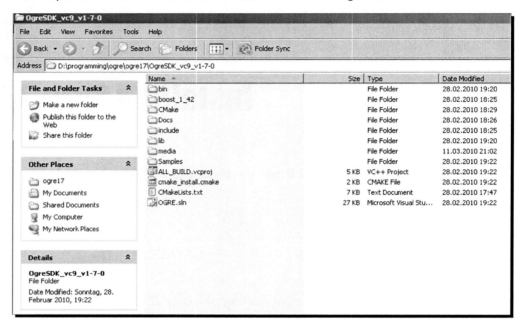

What just happened?

We just downloaded the appropriate Ogre 3D SDK for our system. Ogre 3D is a cross-platform render engine, so there are a lot of different packages for these different platforms. After downloading we extracted the Ogre 3D SDK.

Different versions of the Ogre 3D SDK

Ogre supports many different platforms, and because of this, there are a lot of different packages we can download. Ogre 3D has several builds for Windows, one for MacOSX, and one Ubuntu package. There is also a package for MinGW and for the iPhone. If you like, you can download the source code and build Ogre 3D by yourself. This chapter will focus on the Windows pre-build SDK and how to configure your development environment. If you want to use another operating system, you can look at the Ogre 3D Wiki, which can be found at http://www.ogre3d.org/wiki. The wiki contains detailed tutorials on how to set up your development environment for many different platforms. The rest of the book is completely platform independent, so if you want to use another development system, feel free to do so. It won't affect the content of this book besides the configuration and conventions of your build environment.

Exploring the SDK

Before we begin building the samples which come with the SDK, let's take a look at the SDK. We will look at the structure the SDK has on a Windows platform. On Linux or MacOS the structure might look different. First, we open the `bin` folder. There we will see two folders, namely, `debug` and `release`. The same is true for the `lib` directory. The reason is that the Ogre 3D SDK comes with debug and release builds of its libraries and dynamic-linked/shared libraries. This makes it possible to use the debug build during development, so that we can debug our project. When we finish the project, we link our project against the release build to get the full performance of Ogre 3D.

When we open either the `debug` or `release` folder, we will see many `dll` files, some `cfg` files, and two executables (`exe`). The executables are for content creators to update their content files to the new Ogre version, and therefore are not relevant for us.

OgreMeshUpgrader.exe	103 KB	Application	28.02.2010 19:19
OgreXMLConverter.exe	216 KB	Application	28.02.2010 19:20
cg.dll	5.484 KB	Application Extension	29.09.2009 14:31
OgreMain.dll	6.906 KB	Application Extension	28.02.2010 18:37
OgrePaging.dll	163 KB	Application Extension	28.02.2010 18:38
OgreProperty.dll	67 KB	Application Extension	28.02.2010 19:19
OgreRTShaderSystem.dll	618 KB	Application Extension	28.02.2010 18:42
OgreTerrain.dll	341 KB	Application Extension	28.02.2010 18:40
OIS.dll	98 KB	Application Extension	15.02.2010 16:38
Plugin_BSPSceneManager.dll	228 KB	Application Extension	28.02.2010 19:19
Plugin_CgProgramManager.dll	149 KB	Application Extension	28.02.2010 19:19
Plugin_OctreeSceneManager.dll	296 KB	Application Extension	28.02.2010 19:20
Plugin_OctreeZone.dll	224 KB	Application Extension	28.02.2010 18:44
Plugin_ParticleFX.dll	108 KB	Application Extension	28.02.2010 18:43
Plugin_PCZSceneManager.dll	282 KB	Application Extension	28.02.2010 18:42
RenderSystem_Direct3D9.dll	567 KB	Application Extension	28.02.2010 18:42
RenderSystem_GL.dll	737 KB	Application Extension	28.02.2010 18:42
plugins.cfg	1 KB	CFG File	28.02.2010 17:47
quakemap.cfg	1 KB	CFG File	28.02.2010 17:47
resources.cfg	1 KB	CFG File	28.02.2010 17:47
samples.cfg	1 KB	CFG File	28.02.2010 17:47

The `OgreMain.dll` is the most important DLL. It is the compiled Ogre 3D source code we will load later. All DLLs with `Plugin_` at the start of their name are Ogre 3D plugins we can use with Ogre 3D. Ogre 3D plugins are dynamic libraries, which add new functionality to Ogre 3D using the interfaces Ogre 3D offers. This can be practically anything, but often it is used to add features like better particle systems or new scene managers. What these things are will be discussed later. The Ogre 3D community has created many more plugins, most of which can be found in the wiki. The SDK simply includes the most generally used plugins. Later in this book, we will learn how to use some of them. The DLLs with `RenderSystem_` at the start of their name are, surely not surprisingly, wrappers for different render systems that Ogre 3D supports. In this case, these are Direct3D9 and OpenGL. Additional to these two systems, Ogre 3D also has a Direct3D10, Direct3D11, and OpenGL ES(OpenGL for Embedded System) render system.

Besides the executables and the DLLs, we have the `cfg` files. `cfg` files are config files that Ogre 3D can load at startup. `Plugins.cfg` simply lists all plugins Ogre 3D should load at startup. These are typically the Direct3D and OpenGL render systems and some additional `SceneManagers`. `quakemap.cfg` is a config file needed when loading a level in the `Quake3` map format. We don't need this file, but a sample does.

`resources.cfg` contains a list of all resources, like a 3D mesh, a texture, or an animation, which Ogre 3D should load during startup. Ogre 3D can load resources from the file system or from a ZIP file. When we look at `resources.cfg`, we will see the following lines:

```
Zip=../../media/packs/SdkTrays.zip
```

```
FileSystem=../../media/thumbnails
```

`Zip=` means that the resource is in a ZIP file and `FileSystem=` means that we want to load the contents of a folder. `resources.cfg` makes it easy to load new resources or change the path to resources, so it is often used to load resources, especially by the Ogre samples. Speaking of samples, the last `cfg` file in the folder is `samples.cfg`. We don't need to use this `cfg` file. Again, it's a simple list with all the Ogre samples to load for the `SampleBrowser`. But we don't have a `SampleBrowser` yet, so let's build one.

The Ogre 3D samples

Ogre 3D comes with a lot of samples, which show all the kinds of different render effects and techniques Ogre 3D can do. Before we start working on our application, we will take a look at the samples to get a first impression of Ogre's capabilities.

Time for action – building the Ogre 3D samples

To get a first impression of what Ogre 3D can do, we will build the samples and take a look at them.

1. Go to the `Ogre3D` folder.

2. Open the `Ogre3d.sln` solution file.

3. Right-click on the solution and select `Build Solution`.

4. Visual Studio should now start building the samples. This might take some time, so get yourself a cup of tea until the compile process is finished.

5. If everything went well, go into the `Ogre3D/bin` folder.

6. Execute the `SampleBrowser.exe`.

7. You should see the following on your screen:

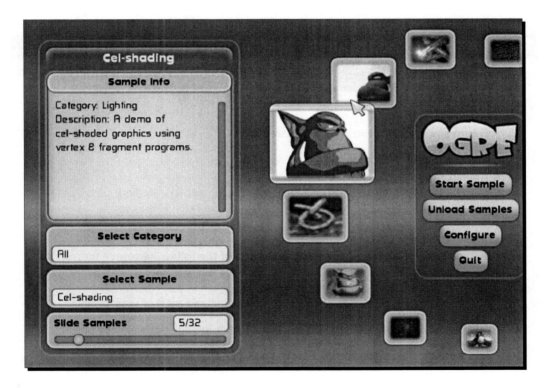

8. Try the different samples to see all the nice features Ogre 3D offers.

What just happened?

We built the Ogre 3D samples using our own Ogre 3D SDK. After this, we are sure to have a working copy of Ogre 3D.

Pop quiz – which post effects are shown in the samples

1. Name at least five different post effects that are shown in the samples.

    a. Bloom, Glass, Old TV, Black and White, and Invert

    b. Bloom, Glass, Old Monitor, Black and White, and Invert

    c. Boom, Glass, Old TV, Color, and Invert

The first application with Ogre 3D

In this part, we will create our first Ogre 3D application, which will simply render one 3D model.

Time for action – starting the project and configuring the IDE

As with any other library, we need to configure our IDE before we can use it with Ogre 3D.

1. Create a new empty project.

2. Create a new file for the code and name it `main.cpp`.

3. Add the main function:

```
int main (void)
{
return 0;
}
```

4. Include `ExampleApplication.h` at the top of the following source file:

```
#include "Ogre\ExampleApplication.h":
```

5. Add `PathToYourOgreSDK\include\` to the include path of your project.

6. Add `PathToYourOgreSDK\boost_1_42` to the include path of your project.

7. Add `PathToYourOgreSDK\boost_1_42\lib` to your library path.

8. Add a new class to the `main.cpp`.

```
class Example1 : public ExampleApplication
{
public:
void createScene()
{
}
};
```

9. Add the following code at the top of your main function:

```
Example1 app;
app.go();
```

10. Add `PathToYourOgreSDK\lib\debug` to your library path.

11. Add `OgreMain_d.lib` to your linked libraries.

12. Add `OIS_d.lib` to your linked libraries.

13. Compile the project.

14. Set your application working directory to `PathToYourOgreSDK\bin\debug`.

15. Start the application. You should see the Ogre 3D Setup dialog.

16. Press **OK** and start the application. You will see a black window. Press *Escape* to exit the application.

What just happened?

We created our first Ogre 3D application. To compile, we needed to set different include and library paths so the compiler could find Ogre 3D.

In steps 5 and 6, we added two include paths to our build environment. The first path was to the Ogre 3D SDK include folder, which holds all the header files of Ogre 3D and OIS. **OIS** stands for **Object Oriented Input System** and is the input library that ExampleApplication uses to process user input. OIS isn't part of Ogre 3D; it's a standalone project and has a different development team behind it. It just comes with Ogre 3D because the ExampleApplication uses it and so the user doesn't need to download the dependency on its own. ExampleApplication.h is also in this include folder. Because Ogre 3D offers threading support, we needed to add the boost folder to our include paths. Otherwise, we can't build any application using Ogre 3D. If needed, Ogre 3D can be built from the source, disabling threading support and thus removing the need for boost. And while using boost, the compiler also needs to be able to link the boost libraries. Thus we have added the boost library folder into our library paths (see step 7).

In step 10, we added PathToYourOgreSDK\lib\debug to our library path. As said before, Ogre 3D comes with debug and release libraries. With this line we decided to use the debug libraries because they offer better debug support if something happens to go wrong. When we want to use the release versions, we have to change the lib\debug to \lib\ release. The same is true for steps 11 und 12. There we added OgreMain_d.lib and OIS_d.lib to our linked libraries. When we want to use the release version, we need to add OgreMain.lib and OIS.lib. OgreMain.lib, and OgreMain_d.lib contains both the interface information about Ogre 3D and tells our application to load OgreMain.dll or OgreMain_d.dll. Note that OIS.lib or OIS_d.lib is the same for the input system—they load OIS_d.dll or OIS.dll. So we link Ogre 3D and OIS dynamically, enabling us to switch the DLL without recompiling our application, as long as the interface of the libraries doesn't change and the application and the DLL are using the same runtime library versions. This also implies that our application always needs to load the DLLs, so we have to make sure it can find it. This is one of the reasons we set the working directory in step 14. Another reason will be made clear in the next section.

ExampleApplication

We created a new class, `Example1`, which inherits from `ExampleApplication`. `ExampleApplication` is a class that comes with the Ogre 3D SDK and is intended to make learning Ogre 3D easier by offering an additional abstraction layer above Ogre 3D. `ExampleApplication` starts Ogre for us, loads different models we can use, and implements a simple camera so we can navigate through our scene. To use `ExampleApplication`, we just needed to inherit from it and override the virtual function `createScene()`. We will use the `ExampleApplication` class for now to save us from a lot of work, until we have a good understanding of Ogre 3D. Later, we will replace `ExamplesApplication` piece-by-piece with our own code.

In the main function, we created a new instance of our application class and called the `go()` function to start the application and load Ogre 3D. At startup, Ogre 3D loads three config files—`Ogre.cfg`, `plugins.cfg`, and `resources.cfg`. If we are using the debug versions, each file needs an "_d" appended to its name. This is useful because with this we can have different configuration files for debug and release. `Ogre.cfg` contains the configuration we selected in the setup dialog, so it can load the same settings to save us from entering the same information every time we start our application. `plugins.cfg` contains a list of plugins Ogre should load. The most important plugins are the `rendersystem` plugins. They are the interface for Ogre to communicate with OpenGL or DirectX to render our scene. `resources.cfg` contains a list of resources that Ogre should load during startup. The Ogre 3D SDK comes with a lot of models and textures we will use in this book and `resources.cfg` points to their location. If you look inside `resources.cfg`, you will see that the paths in this file are relative. That's the reason we need to set the working directory.

Pop quiz – which libraries to link

1. Which libraries do you need to link when using Ogre 3D in release configuration?

    a. OgreD3DRenderSystem.lib

    b. OgreMain.lib

    c. OIS.lib

2. What would we have to change when we want to use the debug build versions of Ogre 3D?

    a. Add an _debug after the library name

    b. Add an _d at the file extension

    c. Add an _d after the library name

Loading the first model

We have a basic application with nothing in it, which is rather boring. Now we will load a model to get a more interesting scene.

Time for action – loading a model

Loading a model is easy. We just need to add two lines of code.

1. Add the following two lines into the empty `createScene()` method:

```
Ogre::Entity* ent =
mSceneMgr->createEntity("MyEntity","Sinbad.mesh");
mSceneMgr->getRootSceneNode()->attachObject(ent);
```

2. Compile your application again.

3. Start your application. You will see a small green figure after starting the application.

4. Navigate the camera with the mouse and WASD until you see the green figure better.

5. Close the application.

What just happened?

With `mSceneMgr->createEntity("MyEntity","Sinbad.mesh");`,we told Ogre that we wanted a new instance of the `Sinbad.mesh` model. `mSceneMgr` is a pointer to the `SceneManager` of Ogre 3D, created for us by the `ExampleApplication`. To create a new entity, Ogre needs to know which model file to use, and we can give a name to the new instance. It is important that the name is unique; it can't be used twice. If this happens, Ogre 3D will throw an exception. If we don't specify a name, Ogre 3D will automatically generate one for us. We will examine this behavior in more detail later.

We now have an instance of a model, and to make it visible, we need to attach it to our scene. Attaching an entity is rather easy—just write the following line:

`mSceneMgr->getRootSceneNode()->attachObject(ent);`

This attaches the entity to our scene so we can see it. And what we see is Sinbad, the mascot model of Ogre 3D. We will see this model a lot during the course of this book.

Pop quiz – ExampleApplication and how to display a model

Describe in your own words how to load a model and how to make it visible.

Summary

We learned how the Ogre 3D SDK is organized, which libraries we needed to link, and which folder we needed in our include path. Also, we got a first glance at the class `ExampleApplication` and how to use it. We loaded a model and displayed it.

Specifically, we covered:

- Which files are important for the development with Ogre 3D, how they interact with each other, and what their purpose is

- What `ExampleApplication` is for: How this class helps to save us work and what happens during the startup of Ogre 3D

- **Model loading**: We learned how we can create a new instance of a model with `createEntity` and one way to attach the new instance to our scene

After this introduction to Ogre 3D, we will learn more about how Ogre 3D organizes scenes and how we can manipulate the scene in the next chapter.

2
The Ogre Scene Graph

This chapter will introduce us to the concept of a scene graph and how we can use its functions to create complex scenes.

In this chapter, we will:

- ◆ Learn the three basic operations in 3D space
- ◆ How a scene graph is organized
- ◆ The different 3D spaces we can operate in

So let's get on with it.

Creating a scene node

In the last chapter, *Chapter 1, Installing Ogre 3D*, we loaded a 3D model and attached it to our scene. Now we will learn how to create a new scene node and attach our 3D model to it.

Time for action – creating a scene node with Ogre 3D

We are going to use the code from *Chapter 1, Installing Ogre 3D* modify it to create a new scene node, and attach it to the scene. We will follow these steps:

1. In the old version of our code, we had the following two lines in the `createScene()` function:

```
Ogre::Entity* ent = mSceneMgr->createEntity("MyEntity","Sinbad.
mesh");
mSceneMgr->getRootSceneNode()->attachObject(ent);
```

2. Replace the last line with the following:

```
Ogre::SceneNode* node = mSceneMgr->createSceneNode("Node1");
```

3. Then add the following two lines; the order of those two lines is irrelevant for the resulting scene:

```
mSceneMgr->getRootSceneNode()->addChild(node);
node->attachObject(ent);
```

4. Compile and start the application.

5. You should see the same screen you get when starting the application from *Chapter 1*.

What just happened?

We created a new scene node named `Node1`. Then we added the scene node to the root scene node. After this, we attached our previously created 3D model to the newly created scene node so it would be visible.

How to work with the RootSceneNode

The call `mSceneMgr->getRootSceneNode()` returns the root scene node. This scene node is a member variable of the scene manager. When we want something to be visible, we need to attach it to the root scene node or a node which is a child or a descendent in any way. In short, there needs to be a chain of child relations from the root node to the node; otherwise it won't be rendered. As the name suggests, the root scene node is the root of the scene. So the entire scene will be, in some way, attached to the root scene node. Ogre 3D uses a so-called scene graph to organize the scene. This graph is like a tree, it has one root, the root scene node, and each node can have children. We already have used this characteristic when we called `mSceneMgr->getRootSceneNode()->addChild(node);`. There we added the created scene node as a child to the root. Directly afterwards, we added another kind of child to the scene node with `node->attachObject(ent);`. Here, we added an entity to the scene node. We have two different kinds of objects we can add to a scene node. Firstly, we have other scene nodes, which can be added as children and have children themselves. Secondly, we have entities that we want rendered. Entities aren't children and can't have children themselves. They are data objects which are associated with the node and can be thought of as leaves of the tree. There are a lot of other things we can add to a scene, like lights, particle systems, and so on. We will later learn what these things are and how to use them. Right now, we only need entities. Our current scene graph looks like the following:

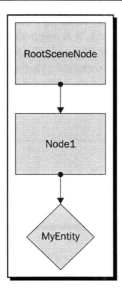

The first thing we need to understand is what a scene graph is and what it does. A scene graph is used to represent how different parts of a scene are related to each other in 3D space.

3D space

Ogre 3D is a 3D rendering engine, so we need to understand some basic 3D concepts. The most basic construct in 3D is a vector, which is represented by an ordered triple (x,y,z).

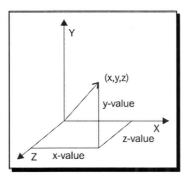

Each position in a 3D space can be represented by such a triple using the Euclidean coordination system for three dimensions. It is important to know that there are different kinds of coordinate systems in 3D space. The only difference between the systems is the orientation of the axis and the positive rotation direction. There are two systems that are widely used, namely, the left-handed and the right-handed versions. In the following image, we see both systems—on the left side, we see the left-handed version; and on the right side, we see the right-handed one.

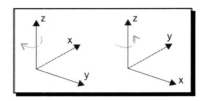

Source: http://en.wikipedia.org/wiki/File:Cartesian_coordinate_system_handedness.svg

The names left-and right-handed are based on the fact that the orientation of the axis can be reconstructed using the left and right hand. The thumb is the x-axis, the index finger the y-axis, and the middle finger the z-axis. We need to hold our hands so that we have a ninety-degree angle between thumb and index finger and also between middle and index finger. When using the right hand, we get a right-handed coordination system. When using the left hand, we get the left-handed version.

Ogre uses the right-handed system, but rotates it so that the positive part of the x-axis is pointing right and the negative part of the x-axis points to the left. The y-axis is pointing up and the z-axis is pointing out of the screen and it is known as the **y-up convention**. This sounds irritating at first, but we will soon learn to think in this coordinate system. The website http://viz.aset.psu.edu/gho/sem_notes/3d_fundamentals/html/3d_coordinates.html contains a rather good picture-based explanation of the different coordination systems and how they relate to each other.

Scene graph

A scene graph is one of the most used concepts in graphics programming. Simply put, it's a way to store information about a scene. We already discussed that a scene graph has a root and is organized like a tree. But we didn't touch on the most important function of a scene graph. Each node of a scene graph has a list of its children as well as a transformation in the 3D space. The transformation is composed of three aspects, namely, the position, the rotation, and the scale. The position is a triple (x,y,z), which obviously describes the position of the node in the scene. The rotation is stored using a quaternion, a mathematical concept for storing rotations in 3D space, but we can think of rotations as a single floating point value for each axis, describing how the node is rotated using radians as units. Scaling is quite easy; again, it uses a triple (x,y,z), and each part of the triple is simply the factor to scale the axis with.

The important thing about a scene graph is that the transformation is relative to the parent of the node. If we modify the orientation of the parent, the children will also be affected by this change. When we move the parent 10 units along the x-axis, all children will also be moved by 10 units along the x-axis. The final orientation of each child is computed using the orientation of all parents. This fact will become clearer with the next diagram.

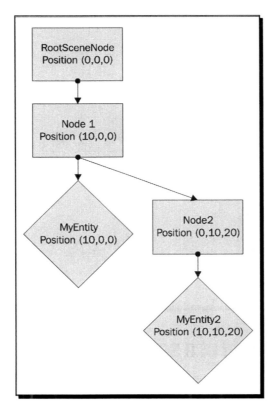

The position of **MyEntity** in this scene will be (**10,0,0**) and **MyEntity2** will be at (**10,10,20**). Let's try this in Ogre 3D.

Pop quiz – finding the position of scene nodes

1. Look at the following tree and determine the end positions of **MyEntity** and **MyEntity2**:

    a. MyEntity(60,60,60) and MyEntity2(0,0,0)

    b. MyEntity(70,50,60) and MyEntity2(10,-10,0)

    c. MyEntity(60,60,60) and MyEntity2(10,10,10)

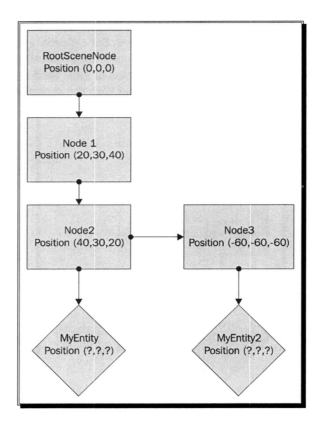

Setting the position of a scene node

Now, we will try to create the setup of the scene from the diagram before the previous image.

Time for action – setting the position of a scene node

1. Add this new line after the creation of the scene node:

   ```
   node->setPosition(10,0,0);
   ```

2. To create a second entity, add this line at the end of the createScene() function:

   ```
   Ogre::Entity* ent2 = mSceneMgr->createEntity("MyEntity2","Sinbad.
   mesh");
   ```

3. Then create a second scene node:

   ```
   Ogre::SceneNode* node2 = mSceneMgr->createSceneNode("Node2");
   ```

4. Add the second node to the first one:

   ```
   node->addChild(node2);
   ```

5. Set the position of the second node:

   ```
   node2->setPosition(0,10,20);
   ```

6. Attach the second entity to the second node:

   ```
   node2->attachObject(ent2);
   ```

7. Compile the program and you should see two instances of Sinbad:

What just happened?

We created a scene which matches the preceding diagram. The first new function we used was at step 1. Easily guessed, the function `setPosition(x,y,z)` sets the position of the node to the given triple. Keep in mind that this position is relative to the parent. We wanted `MyEntity2` to be at (`10,10,20`), because we added `node2`, which holds `MyEntity2`, to a scene node which already was at the position (`10,0,0`). We only needed to set the position of `node2` to (`0,10,20`). When both positions combine, `MyEntity2` will be at (`10,10,20`).

Pop quiz – playing with scene nodes

1. We have the scene node `node1` at (`0,20,0`) and we have a child scene node `node2`, which has an entity attached to it. If we want the entity to be rendered at (`10,10,10`), at which position would we need to set `node2`?

   a. (10,10,10)

   b. (10,-10,10)

   c. (-10,10,-10)

Have a go hero – adding a Sinbad

Add a third instance of Sinbad and let it be rendered at the position (`10,10,30`).

Rotating a scene node

We already know how to set the position of a scene node. Now, we will learn how to rotate a scene node and another way to modify the position of a scene node.

Time for action – rotating a scene node

We will use the previous code, but create completely new code for the `createScene()` function.

1. Remove all code from the `createScene()` function.

2. First create an instance of `Sinbad.mesh` and then create a new scene node. Set the position of the scene node to (`10,10,0`), at the end attach the entity to the node, and add the node to the root scene node as a child:

```
Ogre::Entity* ent = mSceneMgr->createEntity("MyEntity","Sinbad.
mesh");
Ogre::SceneNode* node = mSceneMgr->createSceneNode("Node1");
node->setPosition(10,10,0);
```

```
mSceneMgr->getRootSceneNode()->addChild(node);
node->attachObject(ent);
```

3. Again, create a new instance of the model, also a new scene node, and set the position to (`10,0,0`):

```
Ogre::Entity* ent2 = mSceneMgr->createEntity("MyEntity2","Sinbad.
mesh");
Ogre::SceneNode* node2 = mSceneMgr->createSceneNode("Node2");
node->addChild(node2);
node2->setPosition(10,0,0);
```

4. Now add the following two lines to rotate the model and attach the entity to the scene node:

```
node2->pitch(Ogre::Radian(Ogre::Math::HALF_PI));
node2->attachObject(ent2);
```

5. Do the same again, but this time use the function `yaw` instead of the function `pitch` and the `translate` function instead of the `setPosition` function:

```
Ogre::Entity* ent3 = mSceneMgr->createEntity("MyEntity3","Sinbad.
mesh");
Ogre::SceneNode* node3 = mSceneMgr->createSceneNode("Node3",);
node->addChild(node3);
node3->translate(20,0,0);
node3->yaw(Ogre::Degree(90.0f));
node3->attachObject(ent3);
```

6. And the same again with `roll` instead of `yaw` or `pitch`:

```
Ogre::Entity* ent4 = mSceneMgr->createEntity("MyEntity4","Sinbad.
mesh");
Ogre::SceneNode* node4 = mSceneMgr->createSceneNode("Node4");
node->addChild(node4);
node4->setPosition(30,0,0);
node4->roll(Ogre::Radian(Ogre::Math::HALF_PI));
node4->attachObject(ent4);
```

7. Compile and run the program, and you should see the following screenshot:

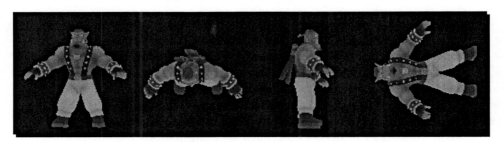

What just happened?

We repeated the code we had before four times and always changed some small details. The first repeat is nothing special. It is just the code we had before and this instance of the model will be our reference model to see what happens to the other three instances we made afterwards.

In step 4, we added one following additional line:

```
node2->pitch(Ogre::Radian(Ogre::Math::HALF_PI));
```

The function `pitch(Ogre::Radian(Ogre::Math::HALF_PI))` rotates a scene node around the x-axis. As said before, this function expects a radian as parameter and we used half of pi, which means a rotation of ninety degrees.

In step 5, we replaced the function call `setPosition(x,y,z)` with `translate(x,y,z)`. The difference between `setPosition(x,y,z)` and `translate(x,y,z)` is that `setPosition` sets the position—no surprises here. `translate` adds the given values to the position of the scene node, so it moves the node relatively to its current position. If a scene node has the position (10,20,30) and we call `setPosition(30,20,10)`, the node will then have the position (30,20,10). On the other hand, if we call `translate(30,20,10)`, the node will have the position (40,40,40). It's a small, but important, difference. Both functions can be useful if used in the correct circumstances, like when we want to position in a scene, we would use the `setPosition(x,y,z)` function. However, when we want to move a node already positioned in the scene, we would use `translate(x,y,z)`.

Also, we replaced `pitch(Ogre::Radian(Ogre::Math::HALF_PI))` with `yaw(Ogre::Degree(90.0f))`. The `yaw()` function rotates the scene node around the y-axis. Instead of `Ogre::Radian()`, we used `Ogre::Degree()`. Of course, `Pitch` and `yaw` still need a radian to be used. However, Ogre 3D offers the class `Degree()`, which has a cast operator so the compiler can automatically cast into a `Radian()`. Therefore, the programmer is free to use a radian or degree to rotate scene nodes. The mandatory use of the classes makes sure that it's always clear which is used, to prevent confusion and possible error sources.

Step 6 introduces the last of the three different rotate function a scene node has, namely, `roll()`. This function rotates the scene node around the z-axis. Again, we could use `roll(Ogre::Degree(90.0f))` instead of `roll(Ogre::Radian(Ogre::Math::HALF_PI))`.

The program when run shows a non-rotated model and all three possible rotations. The left model isn't rotated, the model to the right of the left model is rotated around the x-axis, the model to the left of the right model is rotated around the y-axis, and the right model is rotated around the z-axis. Each of these instances shows the effect of a different rotate function. In short, `pitch()` rotates around the x-axis, `yaw()` around the y-axis, and `roll()` around the z-axis. We can either use `Ogre::Degree(degree)` or `Ogre::Radian(radian)` to specify how much we want to rotate.

Pop quiz – rotating a scene node

1. Which are the three functions to rotate a scene node?

   a. pitch, yawn, roll

   b. pitch, yaw, roll

   c. pitching, yaw, roll

Have a go hero – using Ogre::Degree

Remodel the code we wrote for the previous section in such a way that each occurrence of `Ogre::Radian` is replaced with an `Ogre::Degree` and vice versa, and the rotation is still the same.

Scaling a scene node

We already have covered two of the three basic operations we can use to manipulate our scene graph. Now it's time for the last one, namely, scaling.

Time for action – scaling a scene node

Once again, we start with the same code block we used before.

1. Remove all the code from the `createScene()` function and insert the following code block:

```
Ogre::Entity* ent = mSceneMgr->createEntity("MyEntity","Sinbad.
mesh");
Ogre::SceneNode* node = mSceneMgr->createSceneNode("Node1");
node->setPosition(10,10,0);
mSceneMgr->getRootSceneNode()->addChild(node);
node->attachObject(ent);
```

2. Again, create a new entity:

```
Ogre::Entity* ent2 = mSceneMgr->createEntity("MyEntity2","Sinbad.
mesh");
```

3. Now we use a function that creates the scene node and adds it automatically as a child. Then we do the same thing we did before:

```
Ogre::SceneNode* node2 = node->createChildSceneNode("node2");
node2->setPosition(10,0,0);
node2->attachObject(ent2);
```

4. Now, after the `setPosition()` function, call the following line to scale the model:

```
node2->scale(2.0f,2.0f,2.0f);
```

5. Create a new entity:

```
Ogre::Entity* ent3 = mSceneMgr->createEntity("MyEntity3","Sinbad.
mesh");
```

6. Now we call the same function as in step 3, but with an additional parameter:

```
Ogre::SceneNode* node3 = node->createChildSceneNode("node3",Ogre::
Vector3(20,0,0));
```

7. After the function call, insert this line to scale the model:

```
node3->scale(0.2f,0.2f,0.2f);
```

8. Compile the program and run it, and you should see the following image:

What just happened?

We created a scene with scaled models. Nothing special happened until step 3. Then we used a new function, namely, `node->createChildSceneNode("node2")`. This function is a member function of a scene node and creates a new node with the given name and adds it directly as a child to the node which called the function. In this case, `node2` is added as a child to the node.

In step 4, we used the `scale()` function of the scene node. This function takes a triple (x,y,z), which indicated how the scene node should be scaled. x, y, and z are factors. (0.5,1.0,2.0) means that the scene node should be halved on the x-axis, kept the same on the y-axis, and doubled on the z-axis. Of course, in a really strict sense, the scene node can't be scaled; it only holds metadata which isn't rendered. It would be more precise to say that each renderable object attached to this node would be scaled instead of the scene node itself. The node is only a holder or reference frame for all attached children and renderable objects.

In step 6, we used the `createChildSceneNode()` function again, but this time with more parameters. The second parameter that this function takes is a triple (x,y,z) which is so often used. Ogre 3D has its own class for it called `Ogre::Vector3`. Besides storing the triple, this class offers functions which implement the basic operations. They can be done with three dimensional vectors in linear algebra. This vector describes the translate which should be used when the scene node is created. `createChildSceneNode()` can be used to replace the following lines of code:

```
Ogre::SceneNode* node2 = mSceneMgr->createSceneNode("Node2");
node->addChild(node2);
```

or even

```
Ogre::SceneNode* node2 = mSceneMgr->createSceneNode("Node2");
            node->addChild(node2);
            node2->setPosition(20,0,0);
```

The last piece of code can be replaced with

```
Ogre::SceneNode* node2 = node->createChildSceneNode("Node2",Ogre::
Vector3(20,0,0));
```

If we leave out the `Vector3` parameter, we can replace the first piece of code. There are more versions of this function, which we will use later. If you can't wait, take a look at the documentation of Ogre 3D at `http://www.ogre3d.org/docs/api/html/index.html`.

Besides `scale()`, there is also `setScale()`. The difference between these functions is the same as between `setPosition()` and `translate()`.

Pop quiz – creating child scene nodes

1. Name two different ways of calling `createChildSceneNode()`.

2. How could the following line be replaced without using `createChildSceneNode()`?

   ```
   Ogre::SceneNode* node2 = node->createChildSceneNode("node1",Ogre::
   Vector3(10,20,30));
   ```

    This line could be replaced with three lines. The first creates the scene node, the second one translates it, and the third attaches it to the node.

   ```
   Ogre::SceneNode* node2 = mSceneMgr->createSceneNode("Node2");
   node2->translate(Ogre::Vector3(10,20,30));
   node->addChild(node2);
   ```

Have a go hero – using createChildSceneNode()

Refactor all the code you wrote in this chapter to use `createChildSceneNode()`.

Using a scene graph the clever way

In this section, we will learn how we can use the characteristics of a scene graph to make some tasks easier. This will also expand our knowledge about a scene graph.

Time for action – building a tree using scene nodes

This time, we are going to use another model besides Sinbad: the ninja.

1. Remove all the code from the `createScene()` function.

2. Create Sinbad like we always do:

   ```
   Ogre::Entity* ent = mSceneMgr->createEntity("MyEntity","Sinbad.
   mesh");
   Ogre::SceneNode* node = mSceneMgr->createSceneNode("Node1");
   node->setPosition(10,10,0);
   mSceneMgr->getRootSceneNode()->addChild(node);
   node->attachObject(ent);
   ```

3. Now create a ninja, which will follow Sinbad everywhere he goes:

```
Ogre::Entity* ent2 = mSceneMgr->createEntity("MyEntitysNinja","nin
ja.mesh");
Ogre::SceneNode* node2 = node->createChildSceneNode("node2");
node2->setPosition(10,0,0);
node2->setScale(0.02f,0.02f,0.02f);
node2->attachObject(ent2);
```

4. Compile and run the application. When you take a closer look at Sinbad, you will see a green ninja at his left arm.

5. Now change the position to (40,10,0):

```
node->setPosition(40,10,0);
```

6. And rotate the model 180 degree around the x-axis:

```
node->yaw(Ogre::Degree(180.0f));
```

7. Compile and run the application.

8. You should see that the ninja is still at the left-hand of Sinbad and Sinbad is rotated.

What just happened?

We created a sneaky ninja who follows each step of Sinbad. We made this possible because we added the node the ninja model is attached to as a child to the scene node Sinbad is attached to. When we moved Sinbad, we used his scene node, so each transform we did is also done to the ninja, because this scene node is the child of the node we modify, and as said before, the transformation of a parent is passed to all its children. This fact about scene nodes is extremely helpful to create the following models or complex scenes. Say, if we wanted to create a truck which carries a complete house, we could create the house using a lot of different models and scene nodes. At the end, we would have a scene node where the whole house and its interior are added as children too. Now when we want to move the house, we simply attach the house node to the truck or anything else, and if the truck moves, the complete house moves with it.

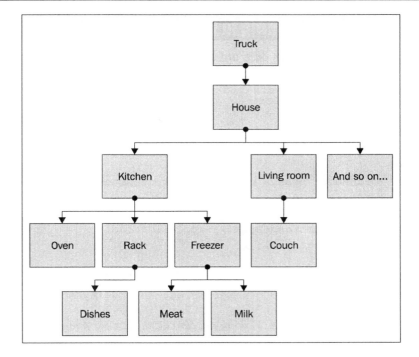

The arrows show the direction the transformations are propagated along the scene graph.

Pop quiz – even more about the scene graph

1. How is transformation information passed in a scene graph?
   a. From the leaves to the root
   b. From the root to the leaves

Have a go hero – adding a following ninja

Add a second ninja to the scene, which follows the first ninja.

Different spaces in a scene

In this part, we will learn that there are different spaces in a scene and how we can use these spaces.

Time for action – translating in World space

We are going to move an object in a different way from what we are used to.

1. Again, start with an empty `createScene()` function; so delete every code you have in this function.

2. Create a reference object:

```
Ogre::Entity* ent = mSceneMgr->createEntity("MyEntity","Sinbad.
mesh");
Ogre::SceneNode* node = mSceneMgr->createSceneNode("Node1");
node->setPosition(0,0,400);
node->yaw(Ogre::Degree(180.0f));
mSceneMgr->getRootSceneNode()->addChild(node);
node->attachObject(ent);
```

3. Create two new instances of the model and translate each one with (0,0,10):

```
Ogre::Entity* ent2 = mSceneMgr->createEntity("MyEntity2","Sinbad.
mesh");
Ogre::SceneNode* node2 = node->createChildSceneNode("node2");
node2->setPosition(10,0,0);
node2->translate(0,0,10);
node2->attachObject(ent2);

Ogre::Entity* ent3 = mSceneMgr->createEntity("MyEntity3","Sinbad.
mesh");
Ogre::SceneNode* node3 = node->createChildSceneNode("node3");
node3->setPosition(20,0,0);
node3->translate(0,0,10);
node3->attachObject(ent3);
```

4. Compile and run the application. Navigate the camera until you see the previous models like the following:

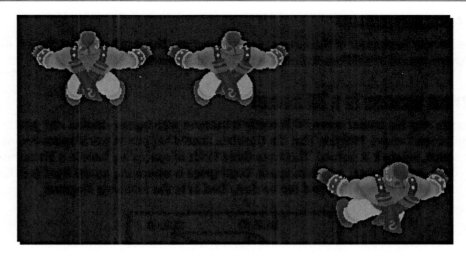

5. Replace the line:

```
node3->translate(0,0,10);
```

with

```
node3->translate(0,0,10,Ogre::Node::TS_WORLD);
```

6. Again, compile and run the application and navigate the camera like before.

What just happened?

We used a new parameter of the `translate()` function. The result was that the left model in the scene moved in a different direction to the middle model.

Different spaces in a 3D scene

The reason why the model moved differently is because with `Ogre::Node::TS_WORLD`, we told the `translate()` function that the translate should happen in world space and not in parent space, where it is normal. There are three kinds of spaces we have in a 3D scene— world space, parent space, and local space. Local space is where the model itself is defined. A cube consists of eight points and can be described as in the following diagram:

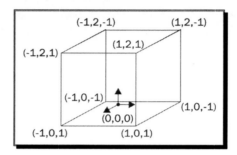

The black point is the null point of local space. Each point of the cube is described as a translate from the null point. When the scene is rendered, the cube needs to be in world space. To get the cube in world space, all transformations of these parents in the scene graph are applied to these points. Let's say the cube is attached to a scene node which is added to the root scene node with a translate of (`10,0,0`). Then the world space with the cube would look like this:

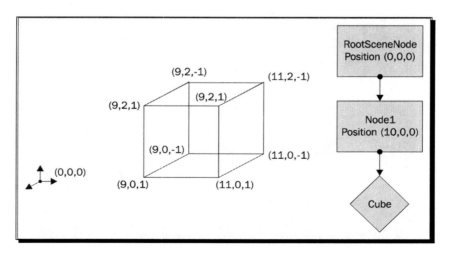

The difference between the two cubes is that the null point has shifted its position, or to be more precise, the cube has been moved away from the null point.

When we call the `translate()` function, the cube is moved in parent space if the space to use is not defined, like we did in step 5. When no parent of the cube is rotated, `translate()` behaves the same way with world space as it would when used with parent or local space. This is true because only the position of the null point changes and not the orientation of the axes. When we, say, move the cube (0,0,10) units, it doesn't matter where the null point is—as long as the axes of the coordination system are orientated the same, it won't change the outcome of the translate process. However, when a parent is rotated, this is no longer true. When the parent is rotated, this also rotates the axis of the null point, which changes the meaning of `translate(0,0,10)`.

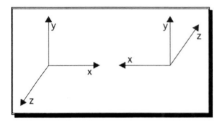

The left coordination system is not rotated and (0,0,10) means moving the cube 10 units nearer to the viewer. This is because the z-axis is pointing out of the screen. With the 180 degree rotation, (0,0,10) means moving the cube 10 units away from the viewer because the z-axis is pointing into the screen.

We see that it is important in what space we describe the `translate()` function to get the desired effect. World space always has the same orientation of axis. To be precise, world spaces uses the left coordination system. Parent space uses a coordination system where all roations from the parent upwards are applied. Local space includes all rotations, from the scene node itself to all parents. The default setting of `translate()` is to use parent space. This enables us to rotate the node itself without changing the direction a node moves when using `translate()`. But there are cases when we want to translate in a space different to parent space. In such cases, we can use the second parameter from `translate()`. The second parameter specifies the space we want the translate to happen in. In our code, we used `Ogre::Node::TS_WORLD` to move the model in world space, which inverted the direction the model used because we rotated the node around 180 degrees, and with this, flipped the direction of the x-and z-axis. Again, look at the image to see the effect.

Translating in local space

We've already seen the effect of translating in parent and world space. Now we will translate in local and parent space to see the difference and get a deeper understanding of the differences between the spaces.

Time for action – translating in local and parent space

1. Clear the `createScene()` function once again.

2. Insert a reference model; this time we will move it nearer to our camera so we don't have to move the camera so much:

    ```
    Ogre::Entity* ent = mSceneMgr->createEntity("MyEntity","Sinbad.
    mesh");
    Ogre::SceneNode* node = mSceneMgr->createSceneNode("Node1");
    node->setPosition(0,0,400);
    node->yaw(Ogre::Degree(180.0f));
    mSceneMgr->getRootSceneNode()->addChild(node);
    node->attachObject(ent);
    ```

3. Add a second model and rotate it by 45 degrees around the y-axis and translate it (0,0,20) units in parent space:

    ```
    Ogre::Entity* ent2 = mSceneMgr->createEntity("MyEntity2","Sinbad.
    mesh");
    Ogre::SceneNode* node2 = node->createChildSceneNode("node2");
    node2->yaw(Ogre::Degree(45));
    node2->translate(0,0,20);
    node2->attachObject(ent2);
    ```

4. Add a third model and also rotate it 45 degrees around the y-axis and translate it (0,0,20) units in local space:

    ```
    Ogre::Entity* ent3 = mSceneMgr->createEntity("MyEntity3","Sinbad.
    mesh");
    Ogre::SceneNode* node3 = node->createChildSceneNode("node3");
    node3->yaw(Ogre::Degree(45));
    node3->translate(0,0,20,Ogre::Node::TS_LOCAL);
    node3->attachObject(ent3);
    ```

5. Compile and run the application. Then navigate the camera again so that you see the model from above.

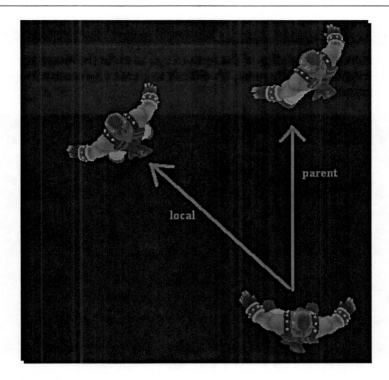

What just happened?

We created our reference model and then added two models which were rotated 45 degrees around the y-axis. Then we translated both with (0,0,20), one model in parent space, the default setting, and the other model in local space. The model we translated in parent space moved in a straight line on the z-axis. But because we rotated the models around the y-axis, the model we translated in local space moved with this rotation and ended up moving up and left in the image. Let's repeat this. When we translate, the default setting is parent space, meaning that all rotations, except the rotation of the scene node we translate, are used while translating. When using world space, no rotation is taken into consideration. When translating, the world coordination system is used. When translating in local space, every rotation, even the rotation from the node we translate, is used for the translation.

Pop quiz – Ogre 3D and spaces

Name three different spaces that Ogre 3D knows.

Have a go hero – adding symmetry

Change the rotation and translation of the `MyEntity2` to make the image symmetric. Make sure you use the right space; otherwise, it's difficult to create a symmetric image. Here is how it should look afterwards:

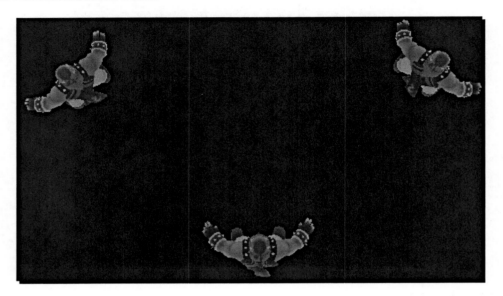

Rotating in different spaces

We have already seen how using different spaces while translating works; we will now do the same with rotating.

Time for action – rotating in different spaces

This time, we are going to rotate using different spaces, as follows:

1. And again, we will start with a clean `createScene()` function, so delete all code inside this function.

2. Add the reference model:

```
Ogre::Entity* ent = mSceneMgr->createEntity("MyEntity","sinbad.
mesh");
Ogre::SceneNode* node = mSceneMgr->createSceneNode("Node1");
mSceneMgr->getRootSceneNode()->addChild(node);
node->attachObject(ent);
```

3. Add a second model and rotate it the normal way:

```
Ogre::Entity* ent2 = mSceneMgr->createEntity("MyEntity2","sinbad.
mesh");
Ogre::SceneNode* node2 = mSceneMgr->getRootSceneNode()-
>createChildSceneNode("Node2");
node2->setPosition(10,0,0);
node2->yaw(Ogre::Degree(90));
node2->roll(Ogre::Degree(90));
node2->attachObject(ent2);
```

4. Add a third model using world space:

```
Ogre::Entity* ent3 = mSceneMgr->createEntity("MyEntity3","Sinbad.
mesh");
Ogre::SceneNode* node3 = node->createChildSceneNode("node3");
node3->setPosition(20,0,0);
node3->yaw(Ogre::Degree(90),Ogre::Node::TS_WORLD);
node3->roll(Ogre::Degree(90),Ogre::Node::TS_WORLD);
node3->attachObject(ent3);
```

5. Compile and run the application.

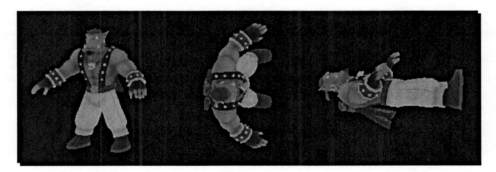

What just happened?

Like always, we created our reference model, which is the left one in the picture. We rotated the second model—first around the y-axis and then around the z-axis. Rotation uses the default space as the local space. This implies that after we rotated the first model 90 degrees around the y-axis, the orientation of z-axis is changed. The second model used the world coordination system and there the orientation of the z-axis stays the same, even when we rotated a scene node.

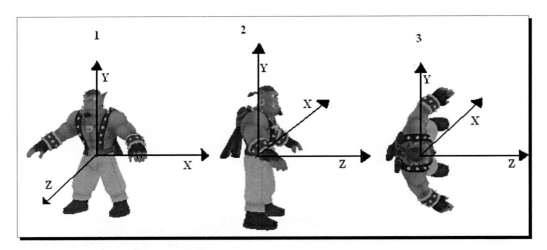

The model under number 1 is the original coordination system we had. Under number 2, we see the coordination system after we rotated 90 degrees around the y-axis. Under number 3, we rotated 90 degrees around the z-axis. Now let's look at the same rotations when we use world space instead of local space.

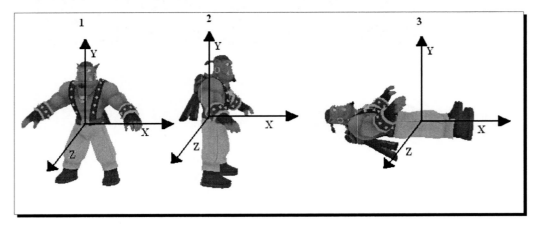

Here we are doing the same rotations, but because we always used world space, we didn't use the changed coordination system, and therefore we got a different result.

Scaling in different spaces

Scaling is always done to the initial model, so there aren't different spaces for scaling. It wouldn't make much sense to scale in different spaces because there isn't really any need to do it.

Summary

We learned a lot in this chapter about the scene graph Ogre 3D uses and how to work with it to create complex scenes.

Specifically, we covered the following:

- What a scene graph is and how it works
- Different ways for changing the position, rotation, and scaling of scene nodes
- What different kinds of spaces we have for rotations and translation
- How we can cleverly use the scene graph's properties to create complex scenes

After being able to create complex scenes in the next chapter, we are going to add light, shadows, and create our own camera.

3
Camera, Light, and Shadow

We already learned how to create a complex scene, but without light and shadow, a scene won't be complete.

In this chapter, we will learn about:

◆ The types of different light sources Ogre 3D supports and how they work

◆ Adding shadows to a scene and the different shadow techniques available

◆ What a camera and viewport are and why we need to have them

Creating a plane

Before we can add lights to our scene, we first need to add a plane, onto which shadows and light are projected, and therefore visible to us. A normal application wouldn't need a plane because there would be a terrain or a floor to project light onto. Light calculation would work without the plane, but we wouldn't be able to see the effect of the light.

Time for action – creating a plane

Until now, we have always loaded a 3D model from a file. Now we will create one directly:

1. Delete all the code inside the `createScene()` function.

2. Add the following line to define a plane in the `createScene()` function:

```
Ogre::Plane plane(Vector3::UNIT_Y, -10);
```

3. Now create the plane into your memory:

```
Ogre::MeshManager::getSingleton().createPlane("plane",
ResourceGroupManager::DEFAULT_RESOURCE_GROUP_NAME, plane,
    1500,1500,20,20,true,1,5,5,Vector3::UNIT_Z);
```

4. Create an instance of the plane:

```
Ogre::Entity* ent = mSceneMgr->createEntity("LightPlaneEntity",
"plane");
```

5. Attach the plane to the scene:

```
mSceneMgr->getRootSceneNode()->createChildSceneNode()-
>attachObject(ent);
```

6. To get anything other than a white plane, set the material of the plane to an existing material:

```
ent->setMaterialName("Examples/BeachStones");
```

7. Compile the application and run it. You should see some dark stones.

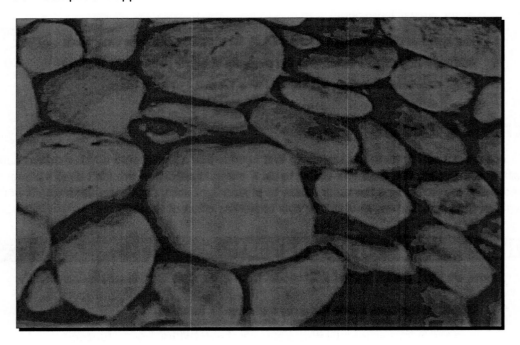

We have inverted the colors for ease of reading!

What just happened?

We just created a plane and added it to the scene. Step 2 created an instance of
`Ogre::Plane`. This class describes a plane using the normal vector of the plane and
an offset from the null point using the normal vector.

A normal vector (or in short, just normal) is an often-used construct in 3D graphics.
The normal of a surface is a vector that stands perpendicular on this surface. The
length of the normal is often 1 and is used extensively in computer graphics for light
and occlusion calculation.

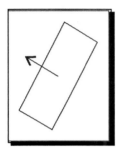

In Step 3, we used the plane definition to create a mesh out of it. To do this, we used
the Ogre `MeshManager`. This manager manages meshes, which shouldn't be a surprise.
Besides managing meshes that we loaded from a file, it can also create planes from our
plane definition, as well as a lot of other things.

```
Ogre::MeshManager::getSingleton().createPlane("plane",
ResourceGroupManager::DEFAULT_RESOURCE_GROUP_NAME, plane,
            1500,1500,20,20,true,1,5,5,Vector3::UNIT_Z);
```

Besides the plane definition, we need to give the plane a name. When loading meshes
from the disk, the file's name is used as the resource name, resource name. It also needs
an resource group it belongs to, resource groups are like namespaces in C++. The third
parameter is the plane definition and the fourth and fifth parameters are the size of the
plane. The sixth and seventh parameters are used to say how many segments the plane
should have. To understand what a segment is, we will take a small detour on how 3D
models are represented in 3D space.

Representing models in 3D

To render a 3D model, it needs to be described in a way a computer can understand and render it most effectively. The most common form to represent 3D models in real-time application is triangles. Our plane can be represented using two triangles to form a quad. With the segment option for the x-and the y-axis, we can control how many triangles are generated for the plane. In the following image, we see the triangles that make up the plane with one, two, or three segments for each axis. To see this effect, we start the application and then press the R key. This will switch the rendering mode first to wireframe mode, where we see the triangles. Another key press will change the mode to point mode, where we see only the points of the triangles. Another press will set the render mode to normal.

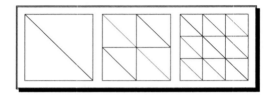

After we have defined how many segments we want, we pass a Boolean parameter which tells Ogre 3D that we want the normal of the plane to be calculated. As said before, a normal is a vector which stands vertically on the surface of the plane. The next three parameters are used for texturing. To texture something all points need texture coordinates. Texture coordinates tell the render engine how to map the texture onto the triangle. Because a picture is a 2D surface, the texture coordinates also consist of two values, namely, x and y. They are presented as a tuple (x,y). The value range of texture coordinates is normalized from zero to one. (0,0) means the upper-left corner of the texture and (1,1) the bottom-right corner. Sometimes the values can be greater than 1. This means that the texture could be repeated depending on the set mode. This topic will be explained in a later chapter extensively. (2,2) could repeat the texture twice across both axis. The tenth and eleventh parameters tell Ogre 3D how often we want the texture to be tiled across the plane. The ninth parameter defines how many textures' coordinates we want. This can be useful when working with more than one texture for one surface. The last parameter defines the "up" direction for our textures. This also affects how the texture coordinates are generated. We simply say that the z-axis should be "up" for our plane.

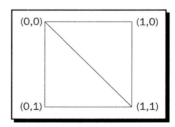

In step 4, we created an instance of the plane that we just created with the `MeshManager`. To do this, we need to use the name we gave the plane during creation. Step 5 attached the entity to the scene.

In step 6, we set a new material to the instance of the entity. Each entity has a material assigned to it. The material describes which texture to use, how the lighting interacts with the material, and much more. We will learn about all of this in the chapter on materials. The plane we created doesn't have a material yet and therefore would be rendered white. Because we want to see the effect of lights we create later, white isn't the best color to use. We used a material that is already defined in the media folder. This material simply adds a stone texture to our plane.

Adding a point light

Now that we have created a plane to see the effect that the light has on our scene, we need to add a light to see something.

Time for action – adding a point light

We will create a point light and add it to our scene to see the effect it has on our scene:

1. Add the following code after setting the material for the plane:

    ```
    Ogre::SceneNode* node = mSceneMgr->createSceneNode("Node1");
    mSceneMgr->getRootSceneNode()->addChild(node);
    ```

2. Create a light with the name `Light1` and tell Ogre 3D it's a point light:

    ```
    Ogre::Light* light1 = mSceneMgr->createLight("Light1");
    light1->setType(Ogre::Light::LT_POINT);
    ```

3. Set the light color and position:

    ```
    light1->setPosition(0,20,0);
    light1->setDiffuseColour(1.0f,1.0f,1.0f);
    ```

4. Create a sphere and set it at the position of the light, so we can see where the light is:

    ```
    Ogre::Entity* LightEnt = mSceneMgr->createEntity("MyEntity","sphere.mesh");
    Ogre::SceneNode* node3 = node->createChildSceneNode("node3");
    node3->setScale(0.1f,0.1f,0.1f);
    node3->setPosition(0,20,0);
    node3->attachObject(LightEnt);
    ```

5. Compile and run the application; you should see the stone texture lit by a white light, and see a white sphere a bit above the plane.

What just happened?

We added a point light to our scene and used a white sphere to mark the position of the light.

In step 1, we created a scene node and added it to the root scene node. We created the scene node because we need it later to attach the light sphere to. The first interesting thing happened in step 2. There we created a new light using the scene manager. Each light will need a unique name, if we decide to give it a name. If we decide not to use a name, then Ogre 3D will generate one for us. We used `Light1` as a name. After creation, we told Ogre 3D that we want to create a point light. There are three different kinds of lights we can create, namely, point lights, spotlights, and directional lights. Here we created a point light; soon we will create the other types of lights. A point light can be thought of as being like a light bulb. It's a point in space which illuminates everything around it. In step 3, we used the created light and set the position of the light and its color. Every light color is described by a tuple (r,g,b). All three parameters have a range from 0.0 to 1.0 and represent the attribution of their assigned color part to the color. 'r' stands for red, 'g' for green, and 'b' for blue. (1.0,1.0,1.0) is white, (1.0,0.0,0.0) is red, and so on. The function we called was `setDiffuseColour(r,g,b)`, which takes exactly these three parameters for the color. Step 4 added a white sphere at the position of the light, so we could see where the light is positioned in the scene.

Have a go hero – adding a second point light

Add a second point light at (20,20,20), which illuminates the scene with a red light. Also add another sphere to show where the point light is. Here's how it should look:

Adding a spotlight

We have created a point light and now we will create a spotlight—the second light type we can use.

Time for action – creating a spotlight

We will use the code we created before and modify it a bit to see how a spotlight works:

1. Delete the code where we created the light and insert the following code to create a new scene node. Be careful not to delete the part of the code we used to create LigthEnt and then add the following code:

    ```
    Ogre::SceneNode* node2 = node->createChildSceneNode("node2");
    node2->setPosition(0,100,0);
    ```

2. Again, create a light, but now set the type to spotlight:

```
Ogre::Light* light = mSceneMgr->createLight("Light1");
light->setType(Ogre::Light::LT_SPOTLIGHT);
```

3. Now set some parameters; we will discuss their meanings later:

```
light->setDirection(Ogre::Vector3(1,-1,0));
light->setSpotlightInnerAngle(Ogre::Degree(5.0f));
light->setSpotlightOuterAngle(Ogre::Degree(45.0f));
light->setSpotlightFalloff(0.0f);
```

4. Set the light color and add the light to the newly created scene node:

```
light->setDiffuseColour(Ogre::ColourValue(0.0f,1.0f,0.0f));
node2->attachObject(light);
```

5. Compile and run the application; it should look like this:

What just happened?

We created a spotlight in the same manner we created a point light; we just used some different parameters for the light.

Step 1 created another scene node to be used later. Step 2 created the light as we did before; we just used a different light type—this time `Ogre::Light::LT_SPOTLIGHT`—to get a spotlight. Step 3 is the really interesting one; there we set different parameters for the spotlight.

Spotlights

Spotlights are just like flashlights in their effect. They have a position where they are and a direction in which they illuminate the scene. This direction was the first thing we set after creating the light. The direction simply defines in which direction the spotlight is pointed. The next two parameters we set were the inner and the outer angles of the spotlight. The inner part of the spotlight illuminates the area with the complete power of the light source's color. The outer part of the cone uses less power to light the illuminated objects. This is done to emulate the effects of a real flashlight. A real flashlight also has an inner part and an outer part that illuminate the area lesser then the center of the spotlight. The inner and outer angles we set define how big the inner and the outer part should be. After setting the angles, we set a `falloff` parameter. This `falloff` parameter describes how much power the light loses when illuminating the outer part of the light cone. The farther away a point to be illuminated is from the inner cone, the more the `falloff` affects the point. If a point is outside the outer cone, then it isn't illuminated by the spotlight.

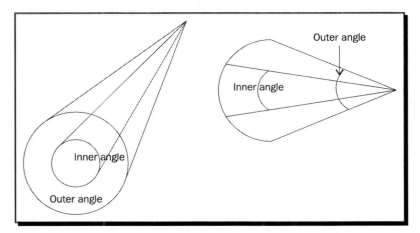

We set the `falloff` to zero. In theory, we should see a perfect light circle on the plane, but it is rather blurry and deformed. The reason for this is that the lighting that we use at the moment uses the triangle points of the plane to calculate and apply the illumination. When creating the plane, we told Ogre 3D that the plane should be created with 20 X 20 segments. This is a rather low resolution for such a big plane and means the light cannot be calculated accurately enough, because there are too few points to apply in an area to make a smooth circle. So to get a better quality render, we have to increase the segments of the plane. Let's say we increase the segments from 20 to 200. The plane creation code looks like this after the increase:

```
Ogre::MeshManager::getSingleton().createPlane("plane",
ResourceGroupManager::DEFAULT_RESOURCE_GROUP_NAME, plane,
1500,1500,200,200,true,1,5,5,Vector3::UNIT_Z);
```

Now when recompiling and restarting the application, we get a nice round circle of light from our spotlight.

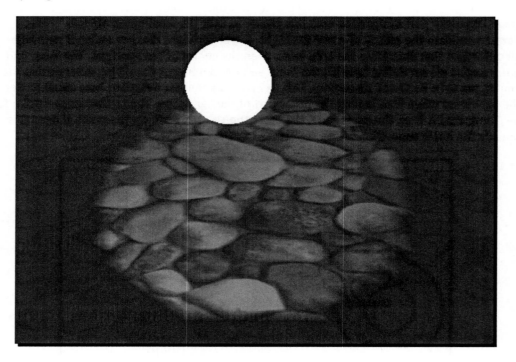

The circle still isn't perfect; if needed, we could increase the segments of the plane even further to make it perfect. There are different lighting techniques which give better results with a low-resolution plane, but they are rather complex and would complicate things now. But even with the complex lighting techniques, the basics are the same and we can change our lighting scheme later using the same lights we created here.

In step 4, we saw another way to describe a color in Ogre 3D. Previously, we used three values, (r,g,b), to set the diffuse color of our light. Here we used `Ogre::ColourValue` (r,g,b), which is basically the same but encapsulated as a class with some additional functions and thus it makes the intention of the parameter clearer.

Pop quiz – different light sources

Describe the difference between a point light and a spotlight in a few words.

Have a go hero – mixing light colors

Create a second spotlight that is at a different position as compared to the first spotlight. Give this spotlight a red color and position it in such a way that the circles of both spotlights overlap each other a bit. You should see that the color is mixing in the area where the green and red light overlap.

Directional lights

We have created spotlights and point lights. Now we are going to create the last light type—directional lights. A directional light is a light that is far away and only has a direction and a color, but no light cone or radius like spotlights or point lights. It can be thought of as the sun. For us, the sunlight comes from one direction, the direction of the sun.

Time for action – creating a directional light

1. Delete all the old code in createScene(), except for the plane-related code.

2. Create a light and set the light type to directional light:
   ```
   Ogre::Light* light = mSceneMgr->createLight("Light1");
   light->setType(Ogre::Light::LT_DIRECTIONAL);
   ```

3. Set the light to a white color and the light direction to shine in a down-right direction:
   ```
   light->setDiffuseColour(Ogre::ColourValue(1.0f,1.0f,1.0f));
   light->setDirection(Ogre::Vector3(1,-1,0));
   ```

4. Compile and run the application.

What just happened?

We created a directional light and set it to shine down and rightwards with setDirection(1,-1,0). In the previous examples, we always had a rather black plane and a small part of the plane was illuminated by our pointlight or spotlight. Here, we used a directional light and hence the complete plane is illuminated. As said before, a directional light can be thought of as the sun, and the sun doesn't have a falloff radius or anything else. So when it shines, it illuminates everything there is; the same is true for our directional light.

Pop quiz – different light types

Recall all three light types that Ogre 3D has and state the differences.

The missing thing

We already have added light to our scene, but something is missing. What's missing will be shown in the next example.

Time for action – finding out what's missing

We are using the previously suggested code to find out what is missing in our scene.

1. After the creation of the light, add code to create an instance of Sinbad.mesh and also create a node and attach the model to it:

```
Ogre::Entity* Sinbad = mSceneMgr->createEntity("Sinbad", "Sinbad.
mesh");
Ogre::SceneNode* SinbadNode = node-
>createChildSceneNode("SinbadNode");
```

2. Then scale Sinbad to three times his size and move him a bit upwards; otherwise, he will be stuck in the plane. Also add him to the scene node, so he will be rendered:

```
SinbadNode->setScale(3.0f,3.0f,3.0f);
SinbadNode->setPosition(Ogre::Vector3(0.0f,4.0f,0.0f));
SinbadNode->attachObject(Sinbad);
```

3. Compile and run the application.

What just happened?

We added an instance of Sinbad into our scene. Our scene is still lit, but we see that Sinbad doesn't throw a shadow, which is rather unrealistic. The next step is to add shadows to our scene.

Adding shadows

Without shadows, a 3D scene isn't really complete; so let's add them.

Time for action – adding shadows

Use the previously used code.

1. After adding all the other code in the `createScene()` function, add the following line:

   ```
   mSceneMgr->setShadowTechnique(Ogre:: SHADOWTYPE_STENCIL_ADDITIVE);
   ```

2. Compile and run the application.

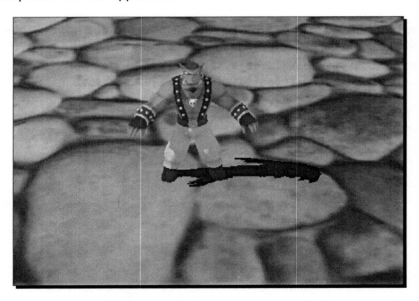

What just happened?

With just one line, we added shadows to our scene. Ogre 3D does the rest of the work for us. Ogre 3D supports different shadow techniques. We used additive stencil shadows. Stencil means a special texture buffer used while rendering the scene. Additive implies that the scene is rendered once from the camera perspective and the contribution of each light is accumulated into the final render. This technique creates good results but is also really expensive because each light adds another rendering run. We won't go into details on how shadows work because this is a complex field. Many books could be written about this topic, and also, shadow techniques change rapidly and are heavily researched. If you are interested in this topic, you can find interesting articles in the NVIDIA book series GPU Gems, the ShaderX book series, and in the proceedings of the Siggraph conference (`http://www.siggraph.org/`).

Creating a camera

So far, we have always used a camera that was created for use by the `ExampleApplication`. Now let's create one for ourselves. A camera, as the name suggests, captures a part of our scene from a certain position. There can only be one camera active at a particular time because we only have one output medium, that is, our monitor. But it is possible to use several cameras in one scene when each one is rendered after the other.

Time for action – creating a camera

This time we won't modify the `createScene()` function; so just leave it as it is with the Sinbad instance and shadows:

1. Create a new empty function named `createCamera()` in the `ExampleApplication` class:

    ```
    void createCamera() {
    }
    ```

2. Create a new camera named `MyCamera1` and assign it to the member `mCamera`:

    ```
    mCamera = mSceneMgr->createCamera("MyCamera1");
    ```

3. Set the position of the camera and let it look at the null point:

    ```
    mCamera->setPosition(0,100,200);
    mCamera->lookAt(0,0,0);
    mCamera->setNearClipDistance(5);
    ```

4. Now change the render mode to wireframe modus:

```
mCamera->setPolygonMode(Ogre::PM_WIREFRAME);
```

5. Compile and run the application.

What just happened?

We overrode the `createCamera()` function, which initially created a camera and set it to a position. After creation, we set a position and used the `lookat()` function to set the camera up to look at the origin. The next step we did was setting the near clipping distance. A camera can only see parts of a 3D scene, so rendering it completely would be a waste of precious CPU and GPU time. To prevent this, before rendering, large parts of the scene are "cut out" from the scene by the `SceneManager`. Only objects visible to the camera are rendered. This step is called **culling**. Only those objects that are before the near clipping plane and behind the far clipping plane are rendered and then only when they are inside a pyramid; this is called the view frustum of the camera. The view frustum is a pyramid with the top cut off; only those objects that are inside the cut-off pyramid can be seen by the camera. More information can be found at `http://www.lighthouse3d.com/opengl/viewfrustum/`. We set the near clipping plane to 5. When you use a higher-value part of the scene which is near the camera, it will be culled and not visible.

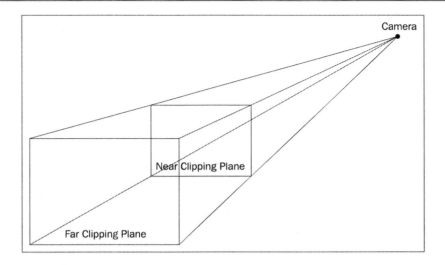

Then we changed the render mode to wireframe. This effect that we get when we press the R key, as suggested before, is the same as the one we got when we wanted to see the plane triangles. With R, this effect can also be undone. When the application starts, we now see a difference as compared to earlier; the camera is now above the instance of Sinbad and looks down on him. Before overriding the createCamera() function, the camera started hovering slightly over the plane looking at the origin. With setPosition(0,100,200), we set the camera higher than before; the following screenshot shows the change.

One interesting aspect we can observe is that even after we have created our own instance of a camera, we can still navigate the scene as before. This is possible because we used the mCamera member variable from ExampleApplication. This keeps ExampleApplication in control of our camera and thus it can be modified. One important feature of a camera is that it can also be attached to a scene node and will react the same way an entity does when attached to a scene node.

Have a go hero – doing more with the thing

Try using different positions and look at points to see how this affects the starting position of the camera.

Also try increasing the near clipping distance and try out what effect this has. This should produce funny images like the following, where we can look into Sinbad's head. The near clipping distance was set to 50 to produce this image.

Creating a viewport

Entwined with the concept of a camera is the concept of a viewport. So we will also create our own viewport. A **viewport** is a 2D surface which is used for rendering. We can think of it as the paper on which a photo is taken. The paper has a background color and if the photo doesn't cover this region, the background color will be seen.

Time for action – doing something that illustrates the thing "in action"

We will use the code that we used before and once again create a new empty method:

1. Remove the `setShadowTechnique()` function call from the `createCamera()` function. We don't want our scene in wireframe mode.

2. Create an empty `createViewports()` method:

```
void createViewports() {
}
```

3. Create a viewport:

```
Ogre::Viewport* vp = mWindow->addViewport(mCamera);
```

4. Set the background color and the aspect ratio:

```
vp->setBackgroundColour(ColourValue(0.0f,0.0f,1.0f));
mCamera->setAspectRatio(Real(vp->getActualWidth()) / Real(vp->getActualHeight()));
```

5. Compile and run the application.

What just happened?

We created a viewport. To do this, we needed to pass a camera to the function. Each viewport can only render the view of one camera, so Ogre 3D enforces that one camera is given during creation. Of course, the camera can be changed later using the appropriate getter and setter functions. The most noticeable change is that the background color changed from black to blue. The reason should be obvious: the new viewport has the background color blue; we set it in step 3. Also in step 3, we set the aspect ratio—the aspect ratio describes the ratio between the width and height of a rendered image; in math terms: aspect ratio = width of window divided by height of window.

Have a go hero – playing with different aspect ratio

Try playing with different aspect ratios and see how this affects the image produced. Also change the background color. Here is an image where the width of the aspect ratio is divided by five.

Summary

In this chapter, we added lights and shadows to our scene, created a viewport, and worked with a `viewfrustum`.

Specifically, we covered:

- What lights are and how they can modify the appearance of our scene
- Adding shadows to our scene
- Creating our own camera, frustum, and viewport

In the next chapter, we will learn how to process user input from the keyboard and mouse. We will also learn what a `FrameListener` is and how to use it.

4
Getting User Input and Using the Frame Listener

Until now, we always created scenes which were static and didn't have anything moving in them. We will change this with this chapter.

In this chapter, we will:

- ◆ Learn what a `FrameListener` is
- ◆ Learn how to process user input
- ◆ Combine both concepts to create our own camera control

So let's get on with it...

Preparing a scene

Before adding moving things to our scene, we need a scene to add them to. So let's create a scene.

Time for action – preparing a scene

We will use a slightly different version of the scene from the previous chapter:

1. Delete all code in the `createScene()` and the `createCamera()` functions.

2. Delete the `createViewports()` function.

3. Add a new member variable to the class. This member variable is a pointer to a scene node:

```
private:
Ogre::SceneNode* _SinbadNode;
```

4. Create a plane and add it to the scene using the `createScene()` method:

```
Ogre::Plane plane(Vector3::UNIT_Y, -10);
Ogre::MeshManager::getSingleton().createPlane("plane",
        ResourceGroupManager::DEFAULT_RESOURCE_GROUP_NAME, plane,
        1500,1500,200,200,true,1,5,5,Vector3::UNIT_Z);

Ogre::Entity* ent = mSceneMgr->createEntity("LightPlaneEntity",
"plane");
mSceneMgr->getRootSceneNode()->createChildSceneNode()-
>attachObject(ent);
ent->setMaterialName("Examples/BeachStones");
```

5. Then add a light to the scene:

```
Ogre::Light* light = mSceneMgr->createLight("Light1");
light->setType(Ogre::Light::LT_DIRECTIONAL);
light->setDirection(Ogre::Vector3(1,-1,0));
```

6. We also need an instance of Sinbad; create a node and attach the instance to it:

```
Ogre::SceneNode* node = mSceneMgr->createSceneNode("Node1");
mSceneMgr->getRootSceneNode()->addChild(node);

Ogre::Entity* Sinbad = mSceneMgr->createEntity("Sinbad", "Sinbad.
mesh");
_SinbadNode = node->createChildSceneNode("SinbadNode");
_SinbadNode->setScale(3.0f,3.0f,3.0f);
_SinbadNode->setPosition(Ogre::Vector3(0.0f,4.0f,0.0f));
_SinbadNode->attachObject(Sinbad);
```

7. We also want shadows in this scene; so activate them:

```
mSceneMgr->setShadowTechnique(SHADOWTYPE_STENCIL_ADDITIVE);
```

8. Create a camera and position it at (0,100,200) and let it look at (0,0,0); remember to add the code to the `createCamera()` function:

```
mCamera = mSceneMgr->createCamera("MyCamera1");
mCamera->setPosition(0,100,200);
mCamera->lookAt(0,0,0);
mCamera->setNearClipDistance(5);
```

9. Compile and run the application, and you should see the following image:

What just happened?

We used the knowledge from the previous chapters to create a scene. We should be able to understand what happened. If not, we should go back to the previous chapters and read them again until we understand everything.

Adding movement to the scene

We have created our scene; now let's add movement to the scene.

Time for action – adding movement to the scene

Up until now, we only had one class, namely, `ExampleApplication`. This time we need another one:

1. Create a new class, name it `Example25FrameListener`, and let it inherit publicly from `Ogre::FrameListener`:

```
class Example25FrameListener : public Ogre::FrameListener
{
};
```

2. Add a private member variable, which is an `Ogre::SceneNode` pointer, and name it `_node`:

```
private:
        Ogre::SceneNode* _node;
```

3. Add a public constructor that takes an `Ogre::SceneNode` pointer as a parameter and assigns it to the member node pointer:

```
public:
        Example25FrameListener(Ogre::SceneNode* node)
        {
                _node = node;
        }
```

4. Add a new function called `frameStarted(FrameEvent& evt)`, which translates the member node with (0,0,0.1) and then returns `true`:

```
bool frameStarted(const Ogre::FrameEvent    &evt)
{
        _node->translate(Ogre::Vector3(0.1,0,0));
        return true;
}
```

5. Add a new member variable to hold the pointer to the `FrameListener`, which we will create later:

```
Ogre::FrameListener* FrameListener;
```

6. Add a constructor which inits the pointer with `NULL` and a destructor which destroys the `FrameListener` when the application is closed:

```
Example25()
{
        FrameListener = NULL;
}
~Example25()
{
        if(FrameListener)
        {
        delete FrameListener;
        }
}
```

7. Now create a new function in `ExampleApplication` called `createFrameListener`. In this function, create an instance of the `FrameListener` we defined and add it using `mRoot`:

```
void createFrameListener()
{
        FrameListener = new Example25FrameListener(_SinbadNode);
        mRoot->addFrameListener(FrameListener);
}
```

8. Compile and run the application. You should see the same scene as seen earlier, but this time, the instance of Sinbad moves right and you can't move the camera or close the application with the *Escape* key. To close the application, click the *X* button on the console windows, or if you started the application from a console, you can use *CTRL+C*.

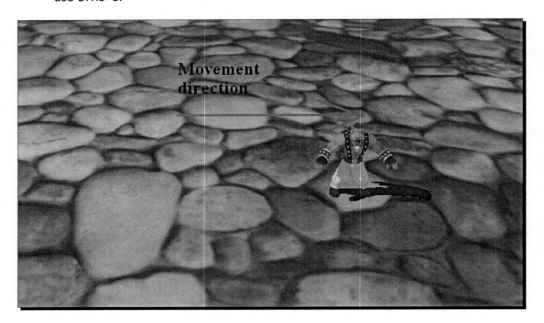

What just happened?

We added a new class to our code which moves our scene node.

FrameListener

The new concept we have encountered here is the concept of FrameListeners. As the name suggests, a FrameListener is based on the observer pattern. We can add a class instance which inherits from the Ogre::FrameListener interface to our Ogre 3D root instance using the addFrameListener() method of Ogre::Root. When this class instance is added, our class gets notified when certain events happen. In this example, we overrode the frameStarted() method. Before a frame (by frame, we mean a single picture of the scene) is rendered, Ogre::Root iterates over all added FrameListeners and calls the frameStarted() method of each one. In our implementation (see step 4) of this function, we translated the node 0.1 units on the x-axis. This node was passed to the Framelistener in its constructor. Therefore, each time the scene is rendered, the node is translated a bit, and as a result, the model moves.

As we have seen during the running of the application, we can't move our camera or exit our application using the *Escape* key. This is because these things were done by the FrameListener, which comes with the ExampleApplication framework. The ExampleApplication framework comes with the SDK. Now that we have replaced it with our own implementation, we can't use the functions the FrameListener offers any longer. But we will reimplement most of them in this chapter, so no worries. If needed, we could still call the functions of the base class to get our default behavior back.

In step 4, our function returns true. If it returned false, Ogre 3D would interpret this as a signal to drop out of the render loop, and with this, the application would be closed. We will use this fact to reimplement the "press *Escape* to exit the application" function.

Pop quiz – design pattern of FrameListener

1. On which design pattern is the FrameListener concept based?

    a. Decorator

    b. Bridge

    c. Observer

Modifying the code to be time based rather than frame based

Depending on your computer, the model in the scene might be moving quite fast or quite slow or just at the right speed. The reason for the different speeds at which the model might move is that, in our code, we move the model 0.1 units on the z-axis before a new frame is rendered every time. A new computer might be able to render the scene with 100 frames per second; this would move the model 10 units per second. When using an old computer, we could have 30 frames per seconds, then the model would only move 3 units. This is only one third, as compared to the new computers. Normally, we want our application to be consistent across different platforms and capabilities so that it will run at the same speed. This can be easily achieved with Ogre.

Time for action – adding time-based movement

We will use the previously used code and only modify one line of code:

1. Change the line where we translate the node to:

```
_node->translate(Ogre::Vector3(10,0,0) * evt.timeSinceLastFrame);
```

2. Compile and run the application. You should see the same scene as before, only the model might move at a different speed.

What just happened?

We changed our movement model from frame-based to time-based. We achieved this by adding a simple multiplication. As said before, frame-based movement has some downfalls. Time-based movement is simply superior because we get the same movement on all computers and have much more control over the movement speed. In step 1, we used the fact that Ogre 3D passes a `FrameEvent` when calling the `frameStarted()` method. This class holds the time since the last frame was rendered in seconds:

```
Ogre::Vector3(10,0,0) * evt.timeSinceLastFrame);
```

This line uses this data to calculate how much we want to move our model in this frame. We use a vector and multiply it by the time since the last frame in seconds. In this case, we will use the vector (10,0,0). This means that we want our model to move 10 units on the x-axis every second. Let's say we render with 10 frames per second; then for each frame, `evt.timeSinceLastFrame` would be 0.1f. In each frame we multiply `evt.timeSinceLastFrame` by the vector (10,0,0), which results in the vector (1,0,0). This result is applied to the scene node of each frame. With 10 frames per second, this will add up to a movement of (10,0,0) per second, which is exactly the value we wanted our model to move by per second.

Pop quiz – the difference between time- and frame-based movement

Describe in your own words the difference between frame-based and time-based movement.

Have a go hero – adding a second model

Add a second model to the scene and let it move in the opposite direction to the current model.

Adding input support

We now have a moving scene, but we would like to be able to exit our application like before. Therefore, we are now going to add input support, and when *Escape* is pressed, we exit our application. Up until now, we only used Ogre 3D; now we will also use **OIS(Object Oriented Input System)**, which comes with the Ogre 3D SDK because it is used by the `ExampleFrameListener`, but otherwise is totally independent from Ogre 3D.

Time for action – adding input support

Again, we use the previous code and add the necessary additions to get input support:

1. We need to add a new parameter to the constructor of our listener. We need a pointer to the render window that Ogre 3D uses to render. To add the new parameter, the code should look like this:

```
Example27FrameListener(Ogre::SceneNode* node,RenderWindow* win)
```

2. When changing the constructor, we also need to change the instantiation:

```
Ogre::FrameListener* FrameListener = new Example27FrameListener(_
SinbadNode,mWindow);
```

3. After this, we need to add code into the constructor of the listener. First, we need two helper variables:

```
size_t windowHnd = 0;
std::stringstream windowHndStr;
```

4. Now ask Ogre 3D for the window handle it renders to:

```
win->getCustomAttribute("WINDOW", &windowHnd);
```

5. Convert the handle into a string:

```
windowHndStr << windowHnd;
```

6. Create a parameter list for OIS and add the window handle to it:

```
OIS::ParamList pl;
pl.insert(std::make_pair(std::string("WINDOW"), windowHndStr.
str()));
```

7. Create the input system using this parameter list:

```
_man = OIS::InputManager::createInputSystem( pl );
```

8. Then create a keyboard so that we can check for user input:

```
_key = static_cast<OIS::Keyboard*>(_man->createInputObject(
OIS::OISKeyboard, false ));
```

9. What we create, we must destroy. Add a destructor to the `FrameListener`, which destroys our created OIS objects:

```
~Example27FrameListener()
{
        _man->destroyInputObject(_key);
```

```
                          OIS::InputManager::destroyInputSystem(_man);
    }
```

10. After we have finished the initialization, add the following code into the
`frameStarted()` method after the node translation and before the return:

```
_key->capture();
if(_key->isKeyDown(OIS::KC_ESCAPE))
{
        return false;
}
```

11. Add the used input objects as member variables to the `FrameListener`:

```
OIS::InputManager* _man;
OIS::Keyboard* _key;
```

12. Compile and run the application. You should now be able to exit the application by
pressing the *Escape* key.

What just happened?

We created an instance of an input system and used this to capture key presses from the
user. Because we need the window handle for the creation of the input system, we changed
the constructor of the `FrameListener` so it gets a pointer to the render window passed.
This was done in step 1. We then converted the handle from a number into a string and
added this string into the parameter list of OIS. With this list, we created our instance of the
input system.

Window handle

A window handle is simply a number that is used as an identifier for a certain window. This
number is created by the operating system and each window has a unique handle. The
input system needs this handle because without it, it couldn't get the input events. Ogre 3D
creates a window for us. So to get the window handle, we need to ask it the following line:

```
win->getCustomAttribute("WINDOW", &windowHnd);
```

There are several attributes that a render window has, so Ogre 3D implements a general getter function. It is also needed to be platform independent; each platform has its own variable types for window handles, so this is the only way for it to be cross platform. WINDOW is the keyword for the window handle. We need to pass to the function a pointer to storage for the handle value; into this pointer the value will be written. After we receive the handle, we convert it into a string using a stringstream because this is what OIS expects. OIS has the same problem and uses the same solution. During creation, we give OIS a list with parameter pairs consisting of an identifier string and a value string. In step 6, we created this parameter list and added the window handle string. Step 7 used this list to create the input system. With the input system, we can create our keyboard interface in step 8. This interface will be used to query the system—which keys are pressed by the user? This is done with the code in step 9. Every time, before we render a frame, we capture the new state of the keyboard using the capture() function. If we didn't call this function, we won't get the newest state of the keyboard and therefore we won't receive any keyboard events ever. After updating the state, we query the keyboard if the escape key is pressed right now. When this is true, we know the user wants to quit the application. This means we must return false to let Ogre 3D know that we want the application to be shut down. Otherwise, if the user wants the application to keep running, we can return true to keep the application running.

Pop quiz – window questions

What is a window handle and how is it used by our application and the operating system?

Adding movement to the model

Now that we have the possibility to get user input, let's use it to control Sinbad's movement on the plane.

Time for action – controlling Sinbad

We use the previous code and add this code where we need, as we did before. We will create a WASD control for Sinbad with the following code:

1. Replace the line where we translate the node in the FrameListener with a zero vector called translate:

   ```
   Ogre::Vector3 translate(0,0,0);
   ```

2. Then add the following keyboard query after the escape query:

   ```
   if(_key->isKeyDown(OIS::KC_W))
   {
           translate += Ogre::Vector3(0,0,-10);
   }
   ```

3. Now add the code to the other three keys. It is basically the same, only the key code and the direction of the vector changes:

```
if(_key->isKeyDown(OIS::KC_S))
{
        translate += Ogre::Vector3(0,0,10);
}
if(_key->isKeyDown(OIS::KC_A))
{
        translate += Ogre::Vector3(-10,0,0);
}
if(_key->isKeyDown(OIS::KC_D))
{
        translate += Ogre::Vector3(10,0,0);
}
```

4. Now use the translate vector to translate the model, and keep in mind to use time-based and not frame-based movement:

```
_node->translate(translate*evt.timeSinceLastFrame);
```

5. Compile and run the application, and you should be able to control Sinbad with the WASD keys

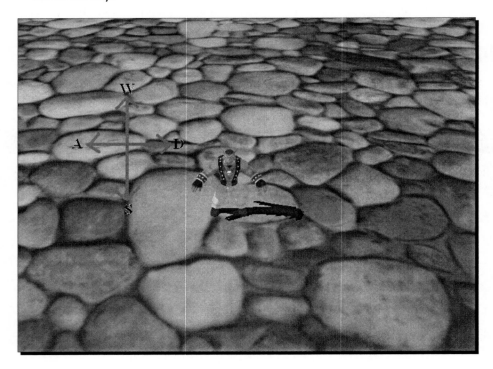

What just happened?

We added a basic movement control using the WASD keys. We queried all four keys and built the accumulative movement vector. We then applied this vector to the model using time-based movement.

Have a go hero – using a speed factor for movement

One downside of this approach is that when we want to change the movement speed of the model, we have to modify four vectors. A better way would be to use the vectors only to indicate the movement direction and use a float variable as the speed factor and multiply the translate vector by it. Change the code to use a movement-speed variable.

Adding a camera

We have our *Escape* key back and we can move Sinbad. Now it's time to get our camera working again.

Time for action – making the camera work again

We have already created our camera; now we are going to use it in combination with user input as follows:

1. Extend the constructor of the `Framelistener` to get a pointer to our camera:

```
Example30FrameListener(Ogre::SceneNode* node,RenderWindow*
win,Ogre::Camera* cam)
```

2. Also add a member variable for storing the camera pointer:

```
Ogre::Camera* _Cam;
```

3. Then assign the parameter to the member:

```
_Cam = cam;
```

4. Modify the instantiation of the `FrameListener` to add the camera pointer:

```
Ogre::FrameListener* FrameListener = new Example30FrameListener(_
SinbadNode,mWindow,mCamera);
```

5. To move the camera, we need to get mouse input. So create a new member variable for storing the mouse:

```
OIS::Mouse* _mouse;
```

6. In the constructor, init the mouse after the keyboard:

```
_mouse = static_cast<OIS::Mouse*>(_man->createInputObject(
OIS::OISMouse, false ));
```

7. Now as we have the mouse, we also need to capture the mouse state as we did with the keyboard. Add this line after the call for capturing the keyboard state:

```
_mouse->capture();
```

8. Remove the line to translate the node:

```
_node->translate(translate*evt.timeSinceLastFrame * _
movementspeed);
```

9. After processing the keyboard state in the `frameStarted()` method, add the following code to process the mouse state:

```
float rotX = _mouse->getMouseState().X.rel * evt.
timeSinceLastFrame* -1;
float rotY = _mouse->getMouseState().Y.rel * evt.
timeSinceLastFrame * -1;
```

10 Now apply the rotations and the translation to the camera:

```
_Cam->yaw(Ogre::Radian(rotX));
_Cam->pitch(Ogre::Radian(rotY));
_Cam->moveRelative(translate*evt.timeSinceLastFrame * _
movementspeed);
```

11 We created a mouse object, so we need to destroy it in the destructor of the `FrameListener`:

```
_man->destroyInputObject(_mouse);
```

12 Compile and run the application. You should be able to navigate the scene, just like we did previously.

What just happened?

We used our created camera in combination with user input. To be able to manipulate the camera, we needed to pass it to our `FrameListener`. This was done in steps 1 and 2 using the constructor. To control our camera, we wanted to use the mouse. So first we had to create a mouse interface to use. This was done in step 6, in the same way we used to create a keyboard. In step 7, we called the `capture()` function of our new mouse interface to update the mouse state.

Mouse state

Querying the keyboard state was done using the `isKeyDown()` function. To get the mouse state, we used the `getMouseState()` function. This function returns a mouse state struct as an instance of the MouseState class, which contains information about the button state, whether they are pressed or not, and how the mouse moved since the last capture call. We want the movement information to calculate how much our camera needs to be rotated. Mouse movement can happen on two axes, namely, the x-axis and the y-axis. Both axes' movements are saved separately in the X and Y variable of the mouse state. We then have the possibility to get the relative or absolute values. Because we are only interested in mouse movement and not the position of the mouse, we are using the relative values. The absolute values contain the position of the mouse on the screen. These are needed when we want to test if the mouse has clicked into a certain area of our application. For camera rotation, we only need the mouse movement, so we use the relative values. The relative value only indicates whether the speed and direction of the mouse has moved, but not the number of pixels.

These values are then multiplied by the time since the last frame and by -1. -1 is used because we get the movement in a different direction to which we want the camera to rotate. So we simply invert the movement direction. After calculating the rotation values, we apply them to the camera with the `yaw()` and `pitch()` functions. The last thing to do is to apply the translation vector we created from the keyboard input to the camera. For this, we use the `moveRelative()` function of the camera. This function translates the camera in the local space without considering the rotation of the camera. This is useful, because we know that in local space (0,0,-1) moves the camera forward. With rotations applied to the camera, this isn't necessarily true. Refer to the chapter about the different spaces in 3D space for a more detailed explanation.

Pop quiz – capturing the input

Why do we call the `capture()` method for the mouse and keyboard?

Have a go hero – playing with the example

Try removing the -1 from the rotation calculation and see how this changes the camera controls.

Try removing the `capture()` function calls and see what impact this has.

Adding wireframe and point render mode

In a previous chapter, that is, Chapter 3, *Camera, Light, and Shadow*, we used the *R* key to change the render mode to wireframe or point rendering. We want to add this feature to our own `framelistener` now.

Time for action – adding wireframe and point render mode

We use the code we just created, and as always, simply add the code we need for this new feature:

1. We need a new member variable in the `framelistener` to save the current render mode:

   ```
   Ogre::PolygonMode _PolyMode;
   ```

2. Init the value in the constructor with PM_SOLID:

   ```
   _PolyMode = Ogre::PolygonMode::PM_SOLID;
   ```

3. We then add a new `if` condition in the `frameStarted()` function, which tests if the *R* key is pressed. If this is the case, we can change the render mode. If the current mode is solid, and we want it to be wireframe:

```
if(_key->isKeyDown(OIS::KC_R))
{
        if(_PolyMode == PM_SOLID)
        {
                _PolyMode = Ogre::PolygonMode::PM_WIREFRAME;
        }
```

4. If it is wireframe, and we want it to change to point mode:

```
else if(_PolyMode == PM_WIREFRAME)
        {
                _PolyMode = Ogre::PolygonMode::PM_POINTS;
        }
```

5. And from point mode, back again to solid:

```
else if(_PolyMode == PM_POINTS)
        {
                _PolyMode = Ogre::PolygonMode::PM_SOLID;
        }
```

6. Now that we have calculated the new render mode, we can apply it and close the `if` condition:

```
_Cam->setPolygonMode(_PolyMode);
}
```

7. Compile and run the application; you should be able to change the render mode by pressing *R*.

What just happened?

We used the function `setPolygonMode()` to change the render mode from solid to wireframe to point. We always saved the last value, so when changing again we know which is the current mode and what the next one will be. We also made sure that we have a circle for the different modes. We changed from solid to wireframe to point and then back to solid. One thing we noticed is that the modes change rather quickly when pressing the *R* key. This is because at each frame we check if the *R* key is pressed and as we humans are slow, chances are high that we press the *R* key longer than one frame. The result is that our application thinks we have pressed the *R* key several times in a short period of time and toggles the wireframe each frame. This isn't optimal and there is a better way to do it, which we will see now.

Adding a timer

A solution for the problem of changing the render mode too fast is the use of a timer. Each time we press the *R* key, a timer is started, and only after enough time has passed, will we process another *R* key press.

Time for action – adding a timer

1. Add the timer as a member variable to the frame listener:

   ```
   Ogre::Timer _timer;
   ```

2. Reset the timer in the constructor:

   ```
   _timer.reset();
   ```

3. Now add a check to see if 0.25 seconds have passed since the last time the *R* key was pressed. Only if that is true, will we continue with processing the input:

   ```
   if(_key->isKeyDown(OIS::KC_R) && _timer.getMilliseconds() > 250)
   {
   ```

4. If enough time has passed, we need to reset the timer; otherwise, the *R* key can only be pressed once:

   ```
   _timer.reset();
   ```

5. Compile and run the application; when pressing the *R* key now, it should only change the render mode to the next one.

What just happened?

We used another new class from Ogre 3D, namely, `Ogre::Timer`. This class offers, as the name suggests, timer functionality. We reset the timer in the constructor of our listener and every time the user presses the *R* key, we check if 0.25 seconds have passed since the last time we called `reset()`. If this is the case, we enter the `if` block and the first thing we do is reset the timer and then change the render mode like before. This makes sure that the render mode is only changed after 0.25 seconds. When we keep pressing the *R* key, we see that our application changes through all render modes with a wait of 0.25 seconds after each change.

Have a go hero – changing the input mode

Change the render mode by changing code in such a way that the mode doesn't change after a certain time has passed, but only when the *R* key is released and pressed again.

Summary

In this chapter, we learned about the `FrameListener` interface and how to use it. We also covered how to start OIS, and after this, how to query the state of the keyboard and mouse interfaces.

Specifically, we covered:

- ◆ How to get notified when a new frame is rendered
- ◆ The important differences between frame- and timed-based movement
- ◆ How to implement our own camera movement using user input
- ◆ How to change the render modes of a camera

Now that we have implemented the basic function for our `FrameListener`, we are going to animate models in the next chapter.

5
Animating models with Ogre 3D

This chapter will focus on animations and how they work in general, and in Ogre 3D specifically. Without animation, a 3D scene is lifeless. It's one of the most important factors for making a scene realistic and interesting.

In this chapter, we will:

◆ Play an animation
◆ Combine two animations at the same time
◆ Attach entities to animations

So let's get on with it...

Adding animations

In the previous chapter, we added interactivity using user input. Now we are going to add another form of interactivity to our scene through animations. Animations are a really important factor for every scene. Without them, every scene looks still and lifeless, but with animations, the scene comes alive. So let's add them.

Time for action – adding animations

As always, we are going to use the code from the previous chapter, and for once we don't need to delete anything:

1. For our animation, we need to add new member variables in the `FrameListener`. Add a pointer holding the entity we want to animate and a pointer to the used animation state:

```
Ogre::Entity* _ent;
Ogre::AnimationState* _aniState;
```

2. Then change the constructor of the `FrameListener` to get the entity pointer as a new parameter:

```
Example34FrameListener(Ogre::SceneNode* node,Ogre::Entity*
ent,RenderWindow* win,Ogre::Camera* cam)
```

3. In the function body of the constructor, assign the given entity pointer to the new member variable:

```
_ent = ent;
```

4. After this, retrieve the animation state called `Dance` from the entity and store it in the member variable we created for this purpose. Finally, set the animation to be enabled and loop it:

```
_aniState = _ent->getAnimationState("Dance");
_aniState->setEnabled(true);
_aniState->setLoop(true);
```

5. Next, we need to tell the animation how much time has passed since it was last updated. We will do this in the `frameStarted()` method; through this we know how much time has passed:

```
_aniState->addTime(evt.timeSinceLastFrame);
```

6. The last thing we need to do is adjust our `ExampleApplication` to work with the new `FrameListener`. Add a new member variable to the application to hold a pointer to the entity:

```
Ogre::Entity* _SinbadEnt;
```

7. Instead of assigning the newly created entity to a local pointer, store it using the member variable. Replace

```
Ogre::Entity* Sinbad = mSceneMgr->createEntity("Sinbad", "Sinbad.
mesh");
```

with

```
_SinbadEnt = mSceneMgr->createEntity("Sinbad", "Sinbad.mesh");
```

8. The same needs to be done when attaching the entity to the node:

```
_SinbadNode->attachObject(_SinbadEnt);
```

9. And of course, when creating the `FrameListener`, add the new parameter to the constructor call:

```
Ogre::FrameListener* FrameListener = new Example34FrameListener(_
SinbadNode,_SinbadEnt,mWindow,mCamera);
```

10. Compile and run the application. You should see Sinbad dancing.

What just happened?

With a few lines of code, we made Sinbad dance. In step 1, we added two new member variables, which will be needed later for animating the model. The first member variable was simply a pointer to the entity we want to animate. The second was a pointer to Ogre::AnimationState, which is used by Ogre 3D for representing a single animation and its associated information. Steps 2 and 3 are straightforward; we changed the constructor to accommodate the new pointer we needed and in step 3 we stored the pointer in the member variables we created in step 1. Interesting stuff happened in step 4; there we asked the entity to return to us the animation named Dance. Each entity stores all the animations it has and we can query them using a string identifier and getAnimationState(). This function returns a pointer to this animation represented as an AnimationState or if the animation doesn't exist, it will return a null pointer. After we got the animation state, we enabled it. This tells Ogre 3D to play this animation. Also, we set the loop property to true so the animation will be played again and again until we stop it. Step 5 is the important one; with this code, we can make the animation come alive. Each time our scene is rendered, we add a bit of time to the animation and therefore Ogre 3D plays it a bit. To be precise, the bit corresponds to the time passed since the last frame. This could, of course, be done by Ogre 3D itself, but this way the function is much more flexible. As an example, we could add a second model which we want to be animated in slow motion. If Ogre 3D updated the animation itself, it could be difficult or impossible for us to animate one model with normal speed and one in slow motion. With the taken approach, we can add a * 0.25 to the time passed since last frame and the model will be animated in slow motion.

The steps after this are simply small modifications of our application so that it is compatible with the changed FrameListener constructor. For this, we needed to save the pointer to the entity we wanted to animate.

Pop quiz – the importance of time

Why do we need to tell Ogre 3D how much time has passed since the animation was last updated and what are the positive side effects of this architecture?

Have a go hero – adding a second model

Add a second model, which stands besides the first one and let it dance in slow motion. You should see two models at different stages of the same animation, as shown in the following image.

Playing two animations at the same time

After adding our first animation, we are going to see why and how it is possible to play two animations at the same time.

Time for action – adding a second animation

Here, we will use the same code that we used for creating the first example:

1. Change the animation from `Dance` to `RunBase`.

```
_aniState = _ent->getAnimationState("RunBase");
```

2. Run and compile the application. You should see Sinbad running, but only with the lower half of his body.

3. For our second animation, we need a new pointer for the animation state:

```
Ogre::AnimationState* _aniStateTop;
```

4. Then, of course, we need to get an animation for this state, enable it, and loop it. The animation we want to get is called `RunTop`:

```
_aniStateTop = _ent->getAnimationState("RunTop");
_aniStateTop->setEnabled(true);
_aniStateTop->setLoop(true);
```

5. The last thing to do is to add the passed time to this animation, like we did for the first one:

```
_aniStateTop->addTime(evt.timeSinceLastFrame);
```

6. Then again run and compile the application. Now you should see Sinbad running with his whole body.

What just happened?

We played two animations at the same time. Before, if you have asked yourself why we needed to get the `AnimationState` to play an animation instead of calling a function like `playAnimation(AnimationName)`, you now have the answer. Ogre 3D supports playing more than one animation at the same time, and with a simple `playAnimation(AnimationName)`, this wouldn't be possible. With animation states, we can play as many animations as we want. We can even play one animation with a different speed than the other, using a modifier variable and the `addTime()` function.

Have a go hero – adding a factor to the animation speed

Add a factor to the top animation and try different values like 0.5 or 4.0 and see how this affects the animation.

Let's walk a bit

We now have a walking animation, but our model doesn't change its position. We will now add basic movement controls to our model and mix them with animations using all the things we have learned.

Time for action – combining user control and animation

And, as always, we will use the previous code as a starting point:

1. Firstly, we need two new variables in the `FrameListener` for controlling the movement speed and saving our rotation:

```
float _WalkingSpeed;
float _rotation;
```

2. In the constructor, we init the new values; we want to move at 50 units per second and start with no rotation:

```
_WalkingSpeed = 50.0f;
_rotation = 0.0f;
```

3. Then we need to change our animation states to prevent them from looping. This time, we are going to control when a new animation has to start and not Ogre 3D:

```
_aniState = _ent->getAnimationState("RunBase");
_aniState->setLoop(false);

_aniStateTop = _ent->getAnimationState("RunTop");
_aniStateTop->setLoop(false);
```

4. In the `frameStarted()` method, we need two new local variables, one to indicate if we have moved our model for this frame and a second one to store the direction in which we have moved our model.

```
bool walked = false;
Ogre::Vector3 SinbadTranslate(0,0,0);
```

5. Also in the `frameStarted()` method, we add some new code to control the movement of our model. We will use the arrow keys for movement. When a key is pressed, we need to change the translation variable to save the direction in which we want to move the model and we need to set the rotation variable to rotate the model in such a way that it looks in the direction it moves:

```
if(_key->isKeyDown(OIS::KC_UP))
{
        SinbadTranslate += Ogre::Vector3(0,0,-1);
        _rotation = 3.14f;
        walked = true;
}
```

6. We need the same for the other three arrow keys:

```
if(_key->isKeyDown(OIS::KC_DOWN))
{
        SinbadTranslate += Ogre::Vector3(0,0,1);
        _rotation = 0.0f;
        walked = true;
}
if(_key->isKeyDown(OIS::KC_LEFT))
{
        SinbadTranslate += Ogre::Vector3(-1,0,0);
        _rotation = -1.57f;
        walked = true;
}
if(_key->isKeyDown(OIS::KC_RIGHT))
{
        SinbadTranslate += Ogre::Vector3(1,0,0);
        _rotation = 1.57f;
        walked = true;
}
```

7. Then, after the key handling, we need to check if we walked this frame. If this is the case, we need to check if the animation has ended. When this is true, we restart the animation:

```
if(walked)
{
        _aniState->setEnabled(true);
        _aniStateTop->setEnabled(true);
        if(_aniState->hasEnded())
        {
                _aniState->setTimePosition(0.0f);
        }
        if(_aniStateTop->hasEnded())
        {
                _aniStateTop->setTimePosition(0.0f);
        }
}
```

8. If we didn't walk this frame, we need to set both animation states to zero. Otherwise, our model would be frozen in an animation half way done and this doesn't look exactly good. So if we don't walk this frame, we set the two animations back to the starting position. Also, we disable both animations since we aren't moving the model of this frame and because we don't need animations:

```
else
{
        _aniState->setTimePosition(0.0f);
        _aniState->setEnabled(false);
        _aniStateTop->setTimePosition(0.0f);
        _aniStateTop->setEnabled(false);
}
```

9. The last thing we need to do is to apply translation and rotation to our model's scene node:

```
_node->translate(SinbadTranslate * evt.timeSinceLastFrame * _
WalkingSpeed);
_node->resetOrientation();
_node->yaw(Ogre::Radian(_rotation));
```

10. Now we compile and run the application. With the mouse and WASD, we can move the camera. With the arrow keys, we can move Sinbad and the right animation gets played each time we move him.

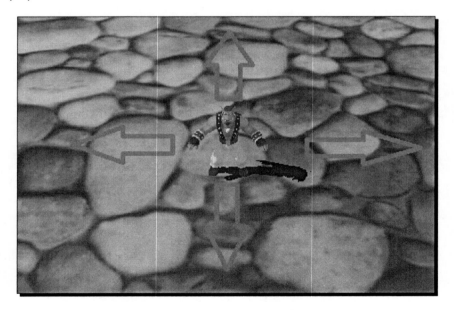

What just happened?

We created our first application with user input and animations combined. This could be called the first real interactive application we created up until now. In steps 1 and 2, we created and inited some variables we needed later. In step 3, we changed how we handle our animations; previously, we always enabled an animation directly and let it loop. Now we don't want to enable it directly because we want the animation only to be played when our model moves, everything else just looks stupid. For the same reason, we disabled looping of animations. We only want to react to user input so that there is no need for animation looping. If needed, we will start the animation ourselves.

Most of the changes we did were inside the `frameStarted()` method. In step 4, we created a couple of local variables we needed later, namely, a Boolean value that was used as an indicator if the model moves this frame and the other was a vector representing the movement direction. Steps 5 and 6 queried the key state of the arrow keys. When a key is down, we change the direction vector and the rotation accordingly and set the flag for movement to `true`. We used this flag in step 7, if the flag is `true`, meaning our model moves this frame, we enabled the animation and checked if the animations had reached their end. If the animations have reached their end, we reset them to their starting position so that they can be played again. Because we don't want animations to be played when the model isn't moving, we set them to their starting position and disable them in step 8. In step 9, we applied the translation. Then we reset the orientation, and after this, applied the new rotation. This is necessary because `yaw` adds the rotation to the already done rotations, which in our case would be wrong because we have absolute rotation, and we need absolute and not relative rotations. Therefore, we reset the orientation first and then apply our rotation to the now zeroed rotation.

Adding swords

We now have a walking, animated model, which can be controlled by user input. Now we are going to see how we can add an object to our animated model.

Time for action – adding swords

As always, we are using the code from our previous excercises:

1. At the end of the `createScene()` function, create two instances of the sword model and name them `Sword1` and `Sword2`:

```
Ogre::Entity* sword1 = mSceneMgr->createEntity("Sword1", "Sword.
mesh");
Ogre::Entity* sword2 = mSceneMgr->createEntity("Sword2", "Sword.
mesh");
```

2. Now attach the sword to the model using a bone name:

```
_SinbadEnt->attachObjectToBone("Handle.L", sword1);
_SinbadEnt->attachObjectToBone("Handle.R", sword2);
```

3. Compile and run the application. There should be two swords in the hands of Sinbad.

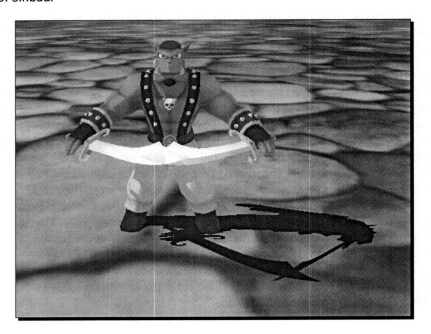

What just happened?

We created two instances of the sword model and attached them to bones. The creation of the instances shouldn't be too difficult to understand. The difficult and interesting part is the function called `attachObjectToBone()`. To understand what this function does, we need to discuss how animations are saved and played.

Animations

For animations, we are using so-called skeletons and bones. The system is inspired by nature; in nature, almost everything has a skeleton to support it. With the help of this skeleton and some muscles, animals and humans can move parts of their body in certain directions. As an example, we can make a fist with our fingers using the joints in our fingers. Animations in computer graphics work in a similar manner. The artist defines the 3D model and for this model a skeleton is created so it can be animated. The skeleton consists of bones and joints. The joints connect two bones and define in which direction the bones can move. Here is a really simplified drawing of such a skeleton; normally, they have a lot more bones.

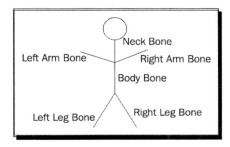

The bones are assigned which triangle they affect when moved. Each bone only affects a part of the model: the bone for the left arm only modifies the triangles of the model which represent the left arm; all other triangles aren't modified.

With joints, bones, and the effect radius of the bones, an artist can create complex animations like the animations for the Sinbad model we are using. Like animations, the bones have names too. Ogre 3D lets us use these bones as a point to attach other entities to. This has the huge advantage that, when attached, the entity gets transformed just like the bone, meaning if we had an attachment point in the hands of Sinbad and attached the swords, they would always be in his hands because when the hands get transformed for an animation, the swords get the same transformation. If this function didn't exist, it would be almost impossible to give models something in their hands or attach things to their backs, like we just did with the swords.

Printing all the animations a model has

We already know that the artist defines the animation names, but sometimes it's important to get the animation names directly from Ogre 3D. This may be needed when you don't have the artist of the model to ask or when you want to check that the export process was successful.

Now we will see how to print all animations of a model into the console.

Time for action – printing all animations

We will use the previous code as base to print all animations that our entity has.

1. At the end of the `createScene()` function, get all the animations that the model has as a set:

```
Ogre::AnimationStateSet* set = _SinbadEnt-
>getAllAnimationStates();
```

2. Then define an iterator and init it with the iterator of the set:

```
Ogre::AnimationStateIterator iter = set-
>getAnimationStateIterator();
```

3. And, finally, iterate over all animations and print their names:

```
while(iter.hasMoreElements())
{
        std::cout << iter.getNext()->getAnimationName() <<
std::endl;
}
```

4. Compile and run the application. After starting the application and loading the scene, you should see the following text in the console of the application:

Dance

DrawSwords

HandsClosed

HandsRelaxed

IdleBase

IdleTop

JumpEnd

JumpLoop

JumpStart

RunBase

RunTop

SliceHorizontal

SliceVertical

What just happened?

We asked the entity to give us a set containing all of the animation it has. We then iterated over this set and printed the name of the animation. We see that there are a lot of animations we didn't use and also some we have already used.

Summary

We learned a lot in this chapter about animation and how to use it to make a 3D scene more interesting.

Specifically, we covered the following:

- How to get an animation from an entity and play it
- How we can enable/disable and loop animations and why we need to tell the animation how much time has passed since the last update
- How we can play two animations at the same time
- How animations are played using a skeleton and that it is possible to attach an entity to a single bone
- How to query an entity for all the animation it contains.

In the next chapter, we are going to see another new aspect of Ogre 3D, mainly that it is possible to use different scene managers and the reason for this.

6
Scene Managers

Ogre 3D offers a lot of functionalities. In this chapter, we are going to touch on some techniques we haven't used before, but ones that are extremely useful for creating complex 3D scenes such as SceneManagers, *creating our own models, speeding up our application, and efficiently rendering large chunks of 3D data.*

In this chapter, we will:

- ◆ Learn how to change the current scene manager
- ◆ Learn what an Octree is
- ◆ Learn how to create our own entities in code
- ◆ Learn how to speed up our application using static geometry

So let's get on with it...

Starting with a blank sheet

This time we are going to use a new blank application and build up from there.

Time for action – creating a blank sheet

1. First we need to include `ExampleApplication`:

```
#include "Ogre\ExampleApplication.h"
```

2. Create a new application class that inherits from `ExampleApplication` and has an empty `createScene()` function:

```
class Example41 : public ExampleApplication
{
public:

        void createScene()
        {

        }

};
```

3. Lastly, we need a main function that creates an instance of the application class and runs it:

```
int main (void)
{
        Example41 app;
        app.go();
        return 0;
}
```

4. Compile this project with the same include and libraries directories as we did previously, and link the same libraries. You should get a black window which can be closed by pressing *Escape*.

What just happened?

We created a new application which inherits from `ExampleApplication` and does nothing. It has an empty `createScene()` function because this is a pure virtual function in the base class and if we don't override it we can't instantiate our class. The more interesting part of the application will be added now.

Getting the scene manager's type

In this following section, we will add a line of code which prints the name and the type of the scene manager we are using.

Time for action – printing the scene manager's type

We are using the previous code as always for the following:

◆ Printing the type and name of the scene manager using the `createScene()` function:

```
std::cout << mSceneMgr->getTypeName() << "::" << mSceneMgr-
>getName() << std::endl;
```

◆ Compiling and running the application. When the application has started to look into the console, there should be the following line:

```
OctreeSceneManager::ExampleSMInstance
```

What just happened?

We added a line which prints the type and name of the `SceneManager`. In this case, the scene manager's name is `ExampleSMInstance`, which is a straightforward name for a scene manger used in the example application. **SM** stands for **Scene Manager**, if you haven't guessed it. The more interesting part is the type, which in this case is `OctreeSceneManager`. Before we go into detail on what an `OctreeSceneManager` is, let's discuss what a scene manager in general does for Ogre 3D.

What does a scene manger do?

A scene manager does a lot of things, which will be obvious when we take a look at the documentation. There are lots of functions which start with create, destroy, get, set, and has. We already used some of these functions, like `createEntity()`, `createLight()`, or `getRootSceneNode()`. One important task the scene manager fulfills is the management of objects. This can be scene nodes, entities, lights, or a lot of other object types that Ogre 3D has. The scene manager acts as a factory for these objects and also destroys them. Ogre 3D works with the principle—*he who creates an object, also destroys it*. Every time we want an entity or scene node deleted, we must use the scene manager; otherwise, Ogre 3D might try to free the same memory later, which might result in an ugly application crash.

Besides object management, it manages a scene, like its name suggests. This can include optimizing the scene and calculating positions of each object in the scene for rendering. It also implements efficient culling algorithms. Each time we move a scene node, it gets flagged as moved. When the scene is rendered, only the position of nodes that have been moved and all their children are calculated. For the rest, we use the positions from the last frame. This saves a lot of computation time and is an important task of the scene manager.

For culling purposes, we need a quick way to discard all nodes that aren't visible from the camera we are using for rendering. This means we need an easy way to traverse the scene graph and test the nodes visibility. There are different algorithms for this and Ogre 3D comes with a different scene manager that implements different algorithms, each specialized for different scene types.

The scene manager we used all the time was the `OctreeSceneManager`. This scene manager uses an Octree for storing the scene, thus the name. So what exactly is an Octree?

Octree

As the name suggests, an **Octree** is a kind of tree. Just like every tree, it has a root and each node has a parent. What makes it special is that each node has a maximum of eight children, hence the name Octree. The following is a diagram showing an Octree:

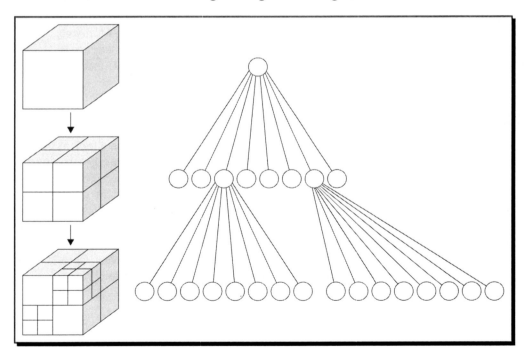

Source: http://commons.wikimedia.org/wiki/File:Octree2.svg

So why does Ogre 3D use an Octree for storing 3D scenes? An Octree has some properties that are extremely useful for storing 3D scenes. One of them is the fact that it can have up to eight children. For example, if we have a 3D scene with two objects in it, we can enclose this scene with a cube.

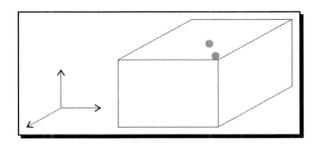

If we divide this cube at half of its width, height, and depth, we get eight new cubes, each enclosing an eighth of the scene. These eight cubes can be thought of as the eight children of the original cube.

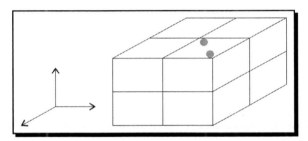

Now the two objects of the scene are in the right upper-front cube. The seven other cubes are empty and are therefore leaves. We will divide the cube that contains the two objects again.

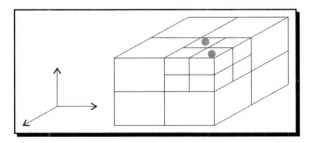

Now each cube has either one or no object enclosed and is a leaf. This property of an Octree makes culling easy and fast. While rendering a scene, we have a camera with its view frustum inside the scene. To determine which objects have to be rendered, we start with the root node of the Octree. If the view frustum intersects the cube, we continue. This should always be the case, because the Octree on level 0 encloses the complete scene with the camera. We then continue with level one of the Octree, meaning the root node's children. We test the view frustum against each child, and if they intersect, we continue with the children of this cube. Also, if the cube is completely inside the frustum, we don't need to go any deeper because we know all children of the cube are in the frustum as well. We do this till we have reached a leaf, and then continue with the next child till we only have leaves left.

With this algorithm, we discard most of a scene with each step, and after only a few steps, we will have either empty leaves or a leaf with an object. We then know which objects are visible and can render them. The beauty of this algorithm is that we can discard a lot of the scene in the first few steps. If, in our example, our complete view frustum would be in the same level 1 cube as the two objects, we could discard seven-eighths of the scene with the first step.

This approach is similar to a binary search tree. The only difference is that it uses eight children instead of two.

Another scene manager type

We have seen one scene manager; now let's look at another one.

Time for action – using another scene manager

Once again, we'll use the code from the previous example:

1. Remove all code inside the `createScene()` function.

2. Add a new function to the application class called `chooseSceneManager()`:

   ```
   virtual void chooseSceneManager(void)
   {
   }
   ```

3. Now add code into the new function to load an archive containing the map we want to be rendered:

   ```
   ResourceGroupManager::getSingleton().addResourceLocation("../../
   media/packs/chiropteraDM.pk3", "Zip", ResourceGroupManager::getSin
   gleton().getWorldResourceGroupName(), true);
   ```

4. After adding the map, we need to load it completely:

```
ResourceGroupManager::getSingleton().initialiseResourceGroup(Resou
rceGroupManager::getSingleton().getWorldResourceGroupName());
```

5. Then we need to use `createSceneManager()`:

```
mSceneMgr = mRoot->createSceneManager("BspSceneManager");
```

6. Now tell the scene manager we want to display the previously loaded map:

```
mSceneMgr->setWorldGeometry("maps/chiropteradm.bsp");
```

7. Compile and run the application. You should see a map from a famous game and be able to navigate through the map. But because the game used a different axis from the up vector, the level will be rotated differently and the navigation can be a bit weird.

What just happened?

We used the `chooseSceneManager()` function to create a scene manager that is different from the default one. In this case, we created a `BspSceneManager`. **BSP** stands for **binary space partition** and is a technique for storing level information used by a lot of old ego shooter games. BSP splits the level into convex parts and stores them as a tree. This makes rendering and other tasks faster on old graphic cards. Nowadays, this isn't necessarily true and BSP isn't used as often as it was some years ago.

ResourceManager

The first line used a new manager we haven't used before called `ResourceGroupManager`. This manager has the responsibility for all assets we load during the lifetime of our application. During startup, the manager gets a list with directories and ZIP archives we want to load. This list can be read from a file, like `resources.cfg`, or it can be written into the application code. After this, we can create an entity using only the filename to create it. We don't need the full path of the file because the manager has already indexed it; only when we create an instance of the index file will it really get loaded. Indexing saves us the trouble of checking that we don't load the same model twice. When we use a model twice, the manager loads each model exactly once, and when we need two instances of the same model, the manager uses the already loaded model and doesn't load it again.

The `addResourceLocation()` function takes a path to a folder or ZIP archive, the second parameter defines which type it is, normally it can either be a zip archive or a folder. We can, if needed also, add our own resource types, and with them, a loader. This is useful when we want to load our own packet format for our assets.

The third parameter is the name of the resource group we want the loaded files to be added to. Resource groups are like namespaces in C++; because we are loading a map, which is part of the game world, we use the predefined resource group name which is returned by `WorldResourceGroup`. The last parameter tells Ogre 3D if we want the path to be loaded with recursion or not. If set to `false`, only the files in the directory will be loaded; files in the subfolder won't be loaded. If set to `true`, Ogre 3D also loads all files in all subfolders. The default is `false`.

With the function call `initialiseResourceGroup()`, we tell Ogre 3D to index all files in the `ResourceGroup` which aren't already indexed. Of course, we have to give the name of the resource group we want to index. After this call, we can use all files that are associated to this `ResourceGroup`.

setWorldGeometry

`setWorldGeometry()` is a special function call telling the `BspSceneManager` to load a map saved in the `bsp` file format. As a map, we use a BSP file that was stored inside the `.pk3` file—that's the reason why we needed to load this archive in the first place.

Creating our own model

We have seen how to use different scene managers and how to load levels using a scene manager. Now we are going to see how to create a mesh in code without the help of the plane class. This time, we will do everything ourselves. We are going to create a model for rendering grass onto our plane.

Time for action – creating a model for displaying blades of grass

This time, we want to use the `OctreeSceneManager`, so we don't need the `chooseSceneManager()` function:

1. We need an empty application:

```cpp
class Example43 : public ExampleApplication
{
private:

public:
      void createScene()
      {

      }
};
```

2. The first thing we need in the `createScene()` function is a plane definition. We will use the plane as our ground for blades of grass:

```
Ogre::Plane plane(Vector3::UNIT_Y, -10);
Ogre::MeshManager::getSingleton().createPlane("plane",
ResourceGroupManager::DEFAULT_RESOURCE_GROUP_NAME, plane,
1500,1500,200,200,true,1,5,5,Vector3::UNIT_Z);
```

3. Then instantiate the newly created plane and set a material. We will use the `GrassFloor` material from the examples:

```
Ogre::Entity* ent = mSceneMgr->createEntity("GrassPlane",
"plane");
mSceneMgr->getRootSceneNode()->createChildSceneNode()-
>attachObject(ent);
ent->setMaterialName("Examples/GrassFloor");
```

4. Then also add a directional light to the scene; otherwise, it would be too dark to see something interesting:

```
Ogre::Light* light = mSceneMgr->createLight("Light1");
light->setType(Ogre::Light::LT_DIRECTIONAL);
light->setDirection(Ogre::Vector3(1,-1,0));
```

5. Now create a new `ManualObject` and call the `begin` method:

```
Ogre::ManualObject*  manual = mSceneMgr-
>createManualObject("grass");
manual->begin("Examples/GrassBlades", RenderOperation::OT_
TRIANGLE_LIST);
```

6. Add the first polygon with the position and texture coordinates for each vertex:

```
manual->position(5.0, 0.0, 0.0);
manual->textureCoord(1,1);
manual->position(-5.0, 10.0, 0.0);
manual->textureCoord(0,0);
manual->position(-5.0, 0.0, 0.0);
manual->textureCoord(0,1);
```

7. We also need a second triangle to make the quad complete:

```
manual->position(5.0, 0.0, 0.0);
manual->textureCoord(1,1);
manual->position(5.0, 10.0, 0.0);
manual->textureCoord(1,0);
manual->position(-5.0, 10.0, 0.0);
manual->textureCoord(0,0);
```

8. We have finished defining the quad; let's tell the manual object:

```
manual->end();
```

9. Lastly, create a new scene node and attach the manual object to it:

```
Ogre::SceneNode* grassNode = mSceneMgr->getRootSceneNode()->create
ChildSceneNode("GrassNode2");
grassNode->attachObject(manual);
```

10. Compile the application and run it. The plane should have a grass texture, and there should be some blades of grass hovering slightly above the plane.

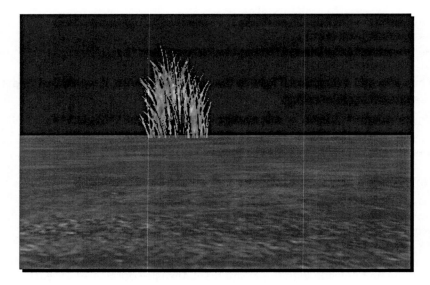

What just happened?

We painted our plane in a different color, this time a grass green; also, we created a quad and put an image of some blades of grass on it. Steps 1 to 4 should be easy to understand, as we have already covered this topic. The only difference is that we used a different material that is more appropriate for the application than the stones we had before. We will cover materials extensively in the next chapter.

In step 5, something new happened. We created a `ManualObject`.

Manual object

A manual object is like a new code file. In the beginning it is empty, but a lot of different things can be created using it. Using a manual object, we can create 3D models. To create one, we need to give single vertices to describe triangles. We have already discussed that all objects we use in a 3D application consist of triangles. But for a quad, we need two triangles, which we will see soon.

Step 5 created a new empty manual object and named it simply as `grass`. We then called the `begin` method, which prepared the manual object to receive its vertex information; a **vertex** is a single point in 3D space. The `begin` method needs a material name that the vertex will be using, the way we are going to input the vertex information, and what we want to create. There are six different ways for how and what we can put into a manual object. There are three different kinds of things we can create with a manual object, namely, points, lines, and triangles.

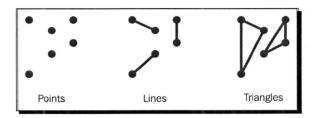

Points are simply stored as a list. Each time we add a new position, we create a new point. This mode is called `OT_POINT_LIST`. For lines, there are two different ways to create them. The straightforward way is to use the first and second position as the first line, the third and fourth position for the second line, and so on. This is called `OT_LINE_LIST`. Another way is to use the first two points as the first line and then each new point defines the end point of a new list and uses the last point as the beginning point for the line; this is an `OT_LINE_STRIP`.

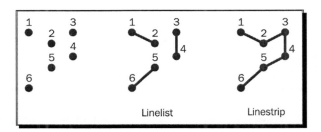

As they are triangles, they can be defined in three ways. The first and simplest way is a triangle list: the first three points are triangle one, the next three are triangle two, and so on. This is known as an `OT_TRIANGLE_LIST`. Then we can use the first three points as the first triangle and each new point defines the next triangle using the last two points of the previous triangle. This is called `OT_TRIANGLE_STRIP`. The last option is to use the first three points for the first triangle and then always the first point and the last-used point with a new point for the next triangle.

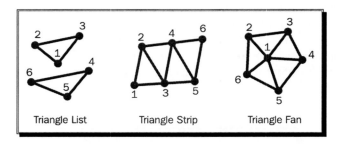

| Triangle List | Triangle Strip | Triangle Fan |

We see that, depending on the input mode, it takes more vertices to describe 3D figures. With a triangle list, we need three points for each triangle. With a strip or fan, we need three for the first and then only one new point for each triangle.

During the begin function call, we defined that we are going to use a triangle list to describe our quad. We want our quad to be 10 units long and 10 units high. Here is an image of the quad; it has four points and each point has its position labeled beside it.

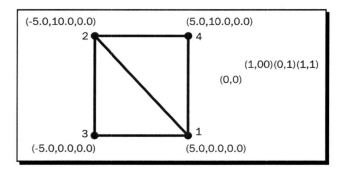

The first triangle needs points 1, 2, and 3. The second triangle needs the points 1, 2, and 4. Step 6 defined the first triangle points with the `position()` function call and step 7 used the `position()` function call to define triangle two. You probably noticed that after each `position()` function call, there was a `textureCoord()` function call.

Texture mapping

For Ogre 3D to be able to put an image of blades of grass onto our quad, each vertex needs texture coordinates besides its position. These consist of two tuples (u,v). (u,v) describes the location in the image, where u is the x-axis and v is the y-axis. (0,0) means the upper-left corner of the image and (1,1) the bottom-right corner.

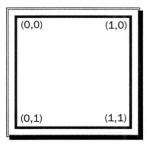

If we use values greater than 1, several effects can happen, depending on the settings in the material. If we use the wrap mode, the texture is repeated. With clamp mode, each value created greater than 1.0 is reduced to 1.0. The same is true for values less than zero—they will be set to zero. In mirror mode, one becomes zero and two becomes one. This mirrors the texture. If the values are greater than two, the original image is used again, after this the flipped, then the original, and so on. The last mode uses the defined border color and everything outside the [0,1] value range is rendered with the border color.

With texture coordinates applied, we have the following information for our quad:

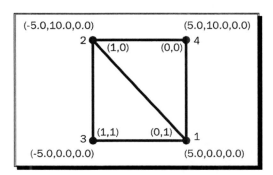

Take a look at steps 6 and 7. Compare the lines of code with the preceding picture. The position and texture coordinates should match.

Step 8 finished our manual object and step 9 created a scene node and attached our object to it so that it gets rendered.

Have a go hero – playing with the manual object

Try the different ways of describing an object using a manual object. Also try lines and points. To make this process easier, use the material `BaseWhiteNoLighting` instead of the grass material. With this material, you don't need texture coordinates, as you can just use the `position()` function and experiment. Everything you create will be rendered as white.

Adding volume to the blades of grass

We have managed to render some blades of grass, but when moving the camera, it quickly becomes clear that the blades are only a 2D image and don't have any volume themselves. This problem can't be easily solved without rendering each blade of grass with our own 3D model, which would improve the visual effect a lot but also is almost impossible because a big grassland would slow the rendering process so much that every interactivity is lost. But there are several techniques to make this problem less problematic. We can see one of them now.

Time for action – using more triangles for volume

We will use the previous code and we will only add two new quads to our grass blades:

1. After the first two triangles, add the third and fourth triangle for the second quad:

```
//third triangle
manual->position(2.5, 0.0, 4.3);
manual->textureCoord(1,1);
manual->position(-2.5, 10.0, -4.3);
manual->textureCoord(0,0);
manual->position(-2.0, 0.0, -4.3);
manual->textureCoord(0,1);

//fourth triangle
manual->position(2.5, 0.0, 4.3);
manual->textureCoord(1,1);
manual->position(2.5, 10.0, 4.3);
manual->textureCoord(1,0);
manual->position(-2.5, 10.0, -4.3);
manual->textureCoord(0,0);
```

2. Add the fifth and sixth triangle for the third quad:

```
//fifth triangle
manual->position(2.5, 0.0, -4.3);
manual->textureCoord(1,1);
manual->position(-2.5, 10.0, 4.3);
manual->textureCoord(0,0);
manual->position(-2.0, 0.0, 4.3);
manual->textureCoord(0,1);

//sixth triangle
manual->position(2.5, 0.0, -4.3);
manual->textureCoord(1,1);
manual->position(2.5, 10.0, -4.3);
manual->textureCoord(1,0);
manual->position(-2.5, 10.0, 4.3);
manual->textureCoord(0,0)
```

3. Compile and run the application, and then navigate around the blades of grass. With the previous examples, it was possible to see the blades of grass only as a small line; this is no longer the case.

BEFORE   AFTER

What just happened?

We fixed the problem where we could see that the blades of grass were only an image projected onto a quad. To fix this problem, we simply created two new quads, rotated them, and then stuck them into each other. It looks like the following diagram:

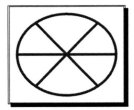

Each quad has the same length, so like the preceding picture, we can think of it as a circle divided into six parts. Between two quads, there is an angle of 60 degrees. Three quads intersecting each other at the center means we have six angles of 60 degrees, making a total of 360 degree. This diagram also answers the only interesting question the previous code could provoke. How did we calculate the new positions of the points for the other two quads? It's simple trigonometry. To calculate the y value, we use sines and for the x value, cosines. This technique that we used creates a plane and renders a texture onto it to simulate a more detailed model, this is a wildly used technique in video games called **billboarding**.

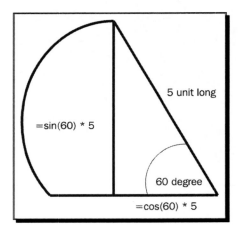

Creating a field of grass

Now that we have one blade of grass, let's build a complete field of grass.

Time for action – building a field of grass

1. We need several instances of our blades of grass, so convert the manual object into a mesh:

```
manual->convertToMesh("BladesOfGrass");
```

2. We want a field of grass which consists of 50 x 50 instances of our grass. So we need two `for` loops:

```
for(int i=0;i<50;i++)
{
        for(int j=0;j<50;j++)
        {
```

3. Inside the `for` loops, create a nameless entity and a nameless scene node:

```
Ogre::Entity * ent = mSceneMgr->createEntity("BladesOfGrass");
Ogre::SceneNode* node = mSceneMgr->getRootSceneNode()->createChild
SceneNode(Ogre::Vector3(i*3,-10,j*3));
node->attachObject(ent);
```

4. Don't forget to close the `for` loops:

```
        }
}
```

5. Compile and run the application, and you should see a field of grass. Depending on your computer, this application might be pretty slow.

What just happened?

In step 1, we used a new function from a manual object which converts the manual object into a mesh we can instantiate using the createEntity() function of the scene manager. To be able to use the new entity, we need a name that will be used later as a parameter for the createEntity() function. We used BladesOfGrass as a descriptive name. We want several instances of our grass, so we created two for loops in step 2, each running 50 times. Step 3 added the body of the for loop. In the body we first created a new entity using the mesh name we just created. An observant reader might notice that we didn't use the createEntity() function with two parameters—one for the entity type and one for the name we want this entity to have. This time, we only gave the entity type as a parameter, not a name. But didn't we have to always give a name to an entity because each entity needs a unique name? This is still true; the function we called is just a helper function, which only needs an entity type name because it generates a unique name and then calls the function we always called. It just saves us the trouble of appending the for loop variables to a generic name like BladesOfGrassEntity. We used the same kind of function for scene node creation.

Exploring the name scheme

Now let's take a quick look at the names Ogre 3D generates for us.

Time for action – printing the names

We only have to add one new line to get the names:

1. At the end of the for loop body, add the following print statement:

    ```
    std::cout << node->getName() << "::" << ent->getName() <<
    std::endl;
    ```

2. Compile and run the application; there should be a long list of printed names. To be precise, there should be 2500 lines, because the for loop iterates 50 times 50 over our code. Here are the last lines:

    Unnamed_2488::Ogre/MO2487

    Unnamed_2489::Ogre/MO2488

    Unnamed_2490::Ogre/MO2489

    Unnamed_2491::Ogre/MO2490

    Unnamed_2492::Ogre/MO2491

    Unnamed_2493::Ogre/MO2492

    Unnamed_2494::Ogre/MO2493

Unnamed_2495::Ogre/MO2494

Unnamed_2496::Ogre/MO2495

Unnamed_2497::Ogre/MO2496

Unnamed_2498::Ogre/MO2497

Unnamed_2499::Ogre/MO2498

Unnamed_2500::Ogre/MO2499

What just happened?

We just printed the names of the scene node and the entity we created to understand the automatic naming scheme Ogre 3D uses when we don't give a name as a parameter. We see that scene node names use the following scheme: Unnamed_Nr, where Nr is a counter that get increased each time we create a new unnamed scene node. Entities use a similar scheme, but they use MO instead of Unnamed_; MO is the short form for movable object. A movable object is a class used as the base class for many different classes in Ogre 3D. Everything that can be moved using scene nodes inherits from a movable object. There are entities and lights, but there are a lot more classes that inherit from a movable object. Here is a picture from the Ogre 3D documentation that shows all the classes which inherit from MovableObject.

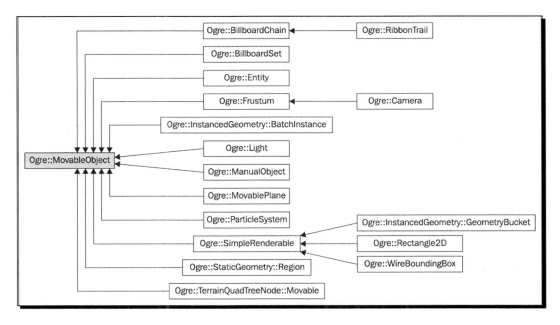

Source: http://www.ogre3d.org/docs/api/html/classOgre_1_1MovableObject.html

We see that even the camera is a movable object; this is necessary because otherwise we wouldn't be able to attach it to a scene node. Only a child class of `MovableObject` can be attached to a scene node. The difference in the numbers attached to the scene nodes names and the movable object names is due to the creation of an unnamed scene node we had done while adding our plane to the scene with the following code:

```
mSceneMgr->getRootSceneNode()->createChildSceneNode()-
>attachObject(ent);
```

Static geometry

We created a field of grass, but the application might be rather slow depending on your computer. We will now make the application faster using an Ogre 3D class called `StaticGeometry`.

Time for action – using static geometry

We are going to modify the code from the last example to make it render faster:

1. Remove the print statement; we don't need it anymore.

2. Now get back to the manual object and remove all `position()` function calls that would add a point we already have added. For each quad, this should be points 4 and 6. Here is the code after removing duplicate entries:

```
manual->position(5.0, 0.0, 0.0);
manual->textureCoord(1,1);
manual->position(-5.0, 10.0, 0.0);
manual->textureCoord(0,0);
manual->position(-5.0, 0.0, 0.0);
manual->textureCoord(0,1);
manual->position(5.0, 10.0, 0.0);
manual->textureCoord(1,0);

manual->position(2.5, 0.0, 4.3);
manual->textureCoord(1,1);
manual->position(-2.5, 10.0, -4.3);
manual->textureCoord(0,0);
manual->position(-2.0, 0.0, -4.3);
manual->textureCoord(0,1);
manual->position(2.5, 10.0, 4.3);
manual->textureCoord(1,0);

manual->position(2.5, 0.0, -4.3);
manual->textureCoord(1,1);
manual->position(-2.5, 10.0, 4.3);
```

```
manual->textureCoord(0,0);
manual->position(-2.0, 0.0, 4.3);
manual->textureCoord(0,1);
manual->position(2.5, 10.0, -4.3);
manual->textureCoord(1,0);
```

3. Now we describe the triangles we want to create using so-called indices. The first quad consists of two triangles; the first triangle uses the first three points and the second triangle uses the first, second, and fourth points. Keep in mind that, like everything else with computers, the points are counted starting with zero:

```
manual->index(0);
manual->index(1);
manual->index(2);

manual->index(0);
manual->index(3);
manual->index(1);
```

4. Add the other two quads the same way:

```
manual->index(4);
manual->index(5);
manual->index(6);

manual->index(4);
manual->index(7);
manual->index(5);

manual->index(8);
manual->index(9);
manual->index(10);

manual->index(8);
manual->index(11);
manual->index(9);
```

5. Now let the `SceneManager` create a new `StaticGeometry` instance:

```
Ogre::StaticGeometry* field = mSceneMgr->createStaticGeometry("Fie
ldOfGrass");
```

6. Now in the `for` loop, create the grass entity. However, this time add it to the static geometry instance instead of the scene node:

```
for(int i=0;i<50;i++)
{
        for(int j=0;j<50;j++)
        {
                Ogre::Entity * ent = mSceneMgr-
>createEntity("BladesOfGrass");
                field->addEntity(ent,Ogre::Vector3(i*3,-10,j*3));

        }
}
```

7. To finish the static geometry, call the build function:

```
field->build();
```

8. Compile and run the application, and you should see the same field of grass, but this time, the application should be a lot faster:

What just happened?

We created the same scene we had before, but this time it runs faster. Why? The sole reason why it runs faster is static geometry. So how does static geometry differ from the "normal" approach we used before?

Rendering pipeline

Each time we are rendering a scene, Ogre 3D and the graphic card has to perform some steps. We have already covered some of them, but not all. One step we covered is culling; now let's discuss some steps we haven't met until now.

We know that there are different spaces an object can be in, like local space or world space. We also know that to render an object, we need to transform them from local space into world space. The transformation from local space to world space is a combination of simple mathematical operations, but they take up some computational time. When rendering our 2,500 grass entities, Ogre 3D has to calculate the world position of every grass entity for each frame. That's a lot of operations per frame, but what's even worse is that each grass entity is sent separately to the GPU for rendering. This takes a lot of time and is the reason why the application is so slow.

We can solve this problem with static geometry; we created an instance of the static geometry class using the scene manager in step 5. However, inside the `for` loop, we added the created entities, not to a scene node like we are used to doing it. Here, we added it directly to the static geometry and gave as a second parameter the position we want the entity to be.

After we finished adding entities to the static geometry instance, we had to call the `build()` function. This function takes all entities we have added and calculates the world position. It does even more. We can only add models that used the indices list because static geometry tries to combine models using the same material or vertex list to optimize itself even more. The price we pay is that we can't move an entity that has been added to static geometry. In the case of our grass field, this isn't a huge trade-off; grass doesn't usually move. Normally, static geometry is used for everything that isn't moving in a scene because it gives a huge speedup with practically no disadvantages. One disadvantage is that when we have a large part of the scene in a static geometry instance, culling is less effective because when one part of the static geometry is inside the view frustum, all of it must be rendered.

Indices

We discovered that we can only add entities that use indices to our static geometry instance. But we haven't discussed what indices are in the first place. To understand this, let's get back to our quad.

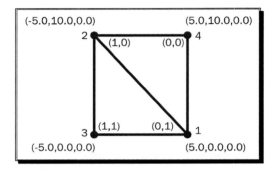

This quad has four points, which define the two triangles the quad is made of. When we look at the code we used to create this quad, we notice that we added six points instead of four and two points are added twice.

```
//First triangle
manual->position(5.0, 0.0, 0.0);
manual->textureCoord(1,1);
manual->position(-5.0, 10.0, 0.0);
manual->textureCoord(0,0);
manual->position(-5.0, 0.0, 0.0);
manual->textureCoord(0,1);

//Second triangle
manual->position(5.0, 0.0, 0.0);
manual->textureCoord(1,1);
manual->position(5.0, 10.0, 0.0);
manual->textureCoord(1,0);
manual->position(-5.0, 10.0, 0.0);
manual->textureCoord(0,0);
```

Points 1 and 2 in the picture are added twice because they are used in both triangles. One way to prevent this information duplication is to use a two-step system for describing triangles. First, we create a list with the points we want to use, and second, we create a list that defines the triangles we want to build out of the points.

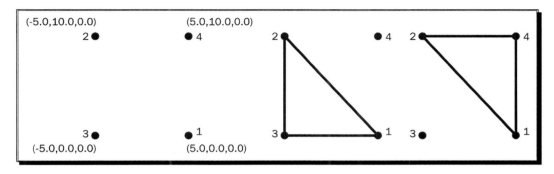

Here we defined four points and then said that triangle one uses points 1, 2 and 3 and triangle two uses points 1, 2, and 4. This saves us from adding some point twice or, even more often, from using them more than twice. Here it may seem like a small difference, but when we have models with several thousand triangles, this really can make a difference. Static geometry demands that we only use entities with indices because, in this way, static geometry can simply create one big list with all points (also known as vertices) and another list with all indices. If we add entities that use the same points, static geometry only needs to add some indices and not new points. For a big level, this can be a huge space saver.

Summary

We have changed the current scene manager, created our own field of grass, and sped up our application with static geometry.

Specifically, we covered:

- What a `ManualObject` is
- Why we use indices for our 3D models
- How and when to use static geometry

We have already used materials in this chapter. In the next chapter, we are going to create our own materials.

7
Materials with Ogre 3D

Without materials, we can't add details to our scene and this chapter is going to give us an introduction to the vast field of using materials.

Materials are a really important topic and it's necessary to understand them to produce good-looking scenes. Materials are also an interesting topic of ongoing research, which has a lot of undiscovered possibilities.

In this chapter, we will:

- ◆ Learn how to create our own materials
- ◆ Apply textures to our quad
- ◆ Understand better how the rendering pipeline works
- ◆ Use the shader to create effects that are impossible without it

So let's get on with it...

Creating a white quad

In the previous chapter, we created our own 3D models with code. Now, we will use this to create a sample quad that we can experiment with.

Time for action – creating the quad

We will start with an empty application and insert the code for our quad into the `createScene()` function:

1. Begin with creating the manual object:

```
Ogre::ManualObject*  manual = mSceneMgr-
>createManualObject("Quad");
manual->begin("BaseWhiteNoLighting", RenderOperation::OT_TRIANGLE_
LIST);
```

2. Create four points for our quad:

```
manual->position(5.0, 0.0, 0.0);
manual->textureCoord(0,1);
manual->position(-5.0, 10.0, 0.0);
manual->textureCoord(1,0);
manual->position(-5.0, 0.0, 0.0);
manual->textureCoord(1,1);
manual->position(5.0, 10.0, 0.0);manual->textureCoord(0,0);
```

3. Use indices to describe the quad:

```
manual->index(0);
manual->index(1);
manual->index(2);

manual->index(0);
manual->index(3);
manual->index(1);
```

4. Finish the manual object and convert it to a mesh:

```
manual->end();
manual->convertToMesh("Quad");
```

5. Create an instance of the entity and attach it to the scene using a scene node:

```
Ogre::Entity * ent = mSceneMgr->createEntity("Quad");
Ogre::SceneNode* node = mSceneMgr->getRootSceneNode()-
>createChildSceneNode("Node1");
node->attachObject(ent);
```

6. Compile and run the application. You should see a white quad.

What just happened?

We used our knowledge from the previous chapter to create a quad and attach to it a material that simply renders everything in white. The next step is to create our own material.

Creating our own material

Always rendering everything in white isn't exactly exciting, so let's create our first material.

Time for action – creating a material

Now, we are going to create our own material using the white quad we created.

1. Change the material name in the application from BaseWhiteNoLighting to MyMaterial1:

   ```
   manual->begin("MyMaterial1", RenderOperation::OT_TRIANGLE_LIST);
   ```

2. Create a new file named Ogre3DBeginnersGuide.material in the media\materials\scripts folder of our Ogre3D SDK.

3. Write the following code into the material file:

   ```
   material MyMaterial1
   {
      technique
      {
         pass
   ```

```
        {
            texture_unit
            {
                texture leaf.png
            }
        }
    }
}
```

4. Compile and run the application. You should see a white quad with a plant drawn onto it.

What just happened?

We created our first material file. In Ogre 3D, materials can be defined in material files. To be able to find our material files, we need to put them in a directory listed in the `resources.cfg`, like the one we used. We also could give the path to the file directly in code using the `ResourceManager`, like we did in the preceding chapter with the map we loaded.

To use our material defined in the material file, we just had to use the name during the begin call of the manual object.

The interesting part is the material file itself.

Materials

Each material starts with the keyword `material`, the name of the material, and then an open curly bracket. To end the material, use a closed curly bracket—this technique should be very familiar to you by now. Each material consists of one or more techniques; a technique describes a way to achieve the desired effect. Because there are a lot of different graphic cards with different capabilities, we can define several techniques and Ogre 3D goes from top to bottom and selects the first technique that is supported by the user's graphic cards. Inside a technique, we can have several passes. A **pass** is a single rendering of your geometry. For most of the materials we are going to create, we only need one pass. However, some more complex materials might need two or three passes, so Ogre 3D enables us to define several passes per technique. In this pass, we only define a texture unit. A **texture unit** defines one texture and its properties. This time the only property we define is the texture to be used. We use `leaf.png` as the image used for our texture. This texture comes with the SDK and is in a folder that gets indexed by `resources.cfg`, so we can use it without any work from our side.

Have a go hero – creating another material

Create a new material called `MyMaterial2` that uses `Water02.jpg` as an image.

Texture coordinates take two

In the previous chapter, we discussed that there are different strategies used when texture coordinates are outside the 0 to 1 range. Now, let's create some materials to see them in action.

Time for action – preparing our quad

We are going to use the quad from the previous example with the leaf texture material:

1. Change the texture coordinates of the quad from range 0 to 1 to 0 to 2. The quad code should then look like this:

```
manual->position(5.0, 0.0, 0.0);
manual->textureCoord(0,2);
manual->position(-5.0, 10.0, 0.0);
manual->textureCoord(2,0);
manual->position(-5.0, 0.0, 0.0);
manual->textureCoord(2,2);
manual->position(5.0, 10.0, 0.0);
manual->textureCoord(0,0);
```

2. Now compile and run the application. Just as before, we will see a quad with a leaf texture, but this time we will see the texture four times.

What just happened?

We simply changed our quad to have texture coordinates that range from zero to two. This means that Ogre 3D needs to use one of its strategies to render texture coordinates that are larger than 1. The default mode is `wrap`. This means each value over 1 is wrapped to be between zero and one. The following is a diagram showing this effect and how the texture coordinates are wrapped. Outside the corners, we see the original texture coordinates and inside the corners, we see the value after the wrapping. Also for better understanding, we see the four texture repetitions with their implicit texture coordinates.

(2,0)			(0,0)
(1,0)	(0,0)	(1,0)	(0,0)
(1,1)	(0,1)	(1,1)	(0,1)
(1,0)	(0,0)	(1,0)	(0,0)
(1,1)	(0,1)	(1,1)	(0,1)
(2,2)			(0,2)

We have seen how our texture gets wrapped using the default texture wrapping mode. Our plant texture shows the effect pretty well, but it doesn't show the usefulness of this technique. Let's use another texture to see the benefits of the wrapping mode.

Using the wrapping mode with another texture

Time for action – adding a rock texture

For this example, we are going to use another texture. Otherwise, we wouldn't see the effect of this texture mode:

1. Create a new material similar to the previous one, except change the used texture to: terr_rock6.jpg:

```
material MyMaterial3
{
    technique
    {
        pass
        {
            texture_unit
            {
```

```
                        texture terr_rock6.jpg
            }
        }
    }
}
```

2. Change the used material from `MyMaterial1` to `MyMaterial3`:

   `manual->begin("MyMaterial3", RenderOperation::OT_TRIANGLE_LIST)`

3. Compile and run the application. You should see a quad covered in a rock texture.

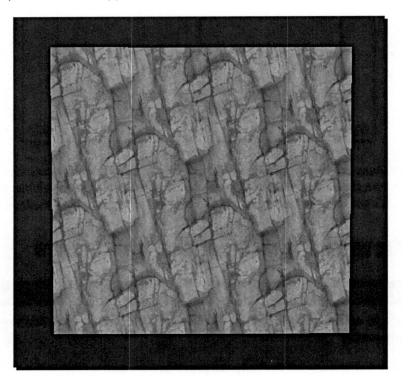

What just happened?

This time, the quad seems like it's covered in one single texture. We don't see any obvious repetitions like we did with the plant texture. The reason for this is that, like we already know, the texture wrapping mode repeats. The texture was created in such a way that at the left end of the texture, the texture is started again with its right side and the same is true for the lower end. This kind of texture is called seamless. The texture we used was prepared so that the left and right side fit perfectly together. The same goes for the upper and lower part of the texture. If this wasn't the case, we would see instances where the texture is repeated.

Using another texture mode

We have seen the effect and usage for the wrapping mode. Now, let's look into another texture mode called clamping.

Time for action – adding a rock texture

We are going to use the same project and just create a new material:

1. Create a new material called MyMaterial4, which is identical to the previous material:

```
material MyMaterial4
{
    technique
    {
        pass
        {
            texture_unit
            {
                texture terr_rock6.jpg
            }
        }
    }
}
```

2. Inside the texture unit block, add a line that tells Ogre 3D to use the clamp mode:

```
tex_address_mode clamp
```

3. Change the material we use for our quad from `MyMaterial3` to `MyMaterial4`:

```
manual->begin("MyMaterial4", RenderOperation::OT_TRIANGLE_LIST);
```

4. Compile and run the application. You should see the stone texture from before in the upper-right corner of the quad. The other three parts of the quad should be lines of different colors.

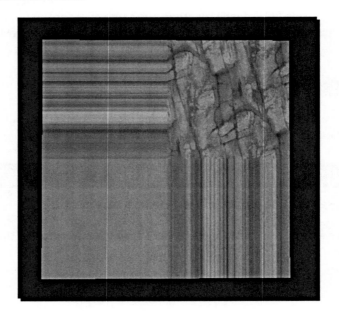

What just happened?

We changed the texture mode to `clamp`. This mode uses the border pixels of a texture to fill all texture coordinates that are greater than 1. In practice, this means the border of an image gets stretched over the model; we can see this effect in the preceding image.

Using the mirror mode

Let's get to the next texture mode that we can use.

Time for action – using the mirror mode

For the `mirror` mode, we again create a new material:

1. Create a new material called `MyMaterial5` using the previous material as a template.

2. Change the texture mode to `mirror`:

   ```
   tex_address_mode mirror
   ```

3. Change the texture to the leaf texture that we used before:

   ```
   texture leaf.png
   ```

4. Compile and run the application, and you should see the leaf mirrored four times.

What just happened?

We again changed the texture mode—this time to mirroring. Mirror is a simple, yet effective, mode when used for texturing big areas like a stone wall. Each time the texture coordinates are bigger than 1, the texture gets flipped and then used as it is in wrap mode. We can see the effect of this in the following diagram.

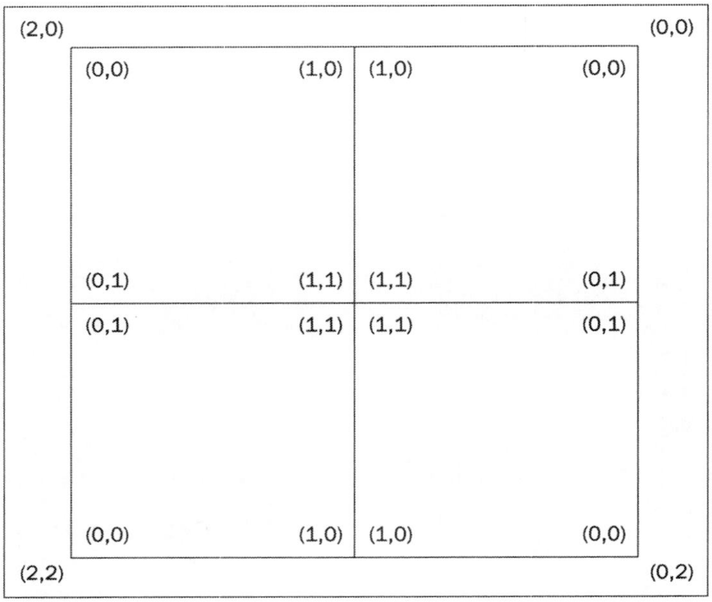

(2,0)			(0,0)
(0,0)	(1,0)	(1,0)	(0,0)
(0,1)	(1,1)	(1,1)	(0,1)
(0,1)	(1,1)	(1,1)	(0,1)
(0,0)	(1,0)	(1,0)	(0,0)
(2,2)			(0,2)

Using the border mode

Only one mode is left for us to try, namely, the border mode.

Time for action – using the border mode

1. Create a new material called MyMaterial6, and just like the previous five times, base it on the material used previously.

2. Change the texture mode to border:

    ```
    tex_address_mode border
    ```

3. Also remember to change the used material in the code file:

    ```
    manual->begin("MyMaterial6", RenderOperation::OT_TRIANGLE_LIST);
    ```

4. Compile and run the application. Surprisingly, this time we will only see one leaf.

What just happened?

Where did the other leaves go? The border mode doesn't create multiple copies of our texture through mirroring or wrapping. When texture coordinates are greater one, this mode paints everything in the defined border color—the default obviously is black, as black can be seen as the zero value for colors.

Changing the border color

If we could only use black as a border color, this feature would be rather useless. Let's see how we can change the border color.

Time for action – changing the border color

1. Copy the last material and name it `MyMaterial7`.

2. After setting the texture mode, add the following line to set the border color to blue:

```
tex_border_color 0.0 0.0 1.0
```

3. Compile and run the application. This time, we also see only one leaf texture, but the rest of the quad should be in blue.

What just happened?

We changed the border color from black to blue. Similarly, we can use any color as the border color, which can be described with an RGB value. This texture mode can be used when putting logos onto objects like racing cars. We only need to set the border color to the color of the car and then add the texture. If there are little errors or inaccuracies with the texture coordinates, they won't show up because the car and the border color are the same.

Pop quiz – texture modes

1. What is the difference between the four texture modes—wrap, clamp, mirror, and border?

    a. How texture coordinates are used which have a value between 0 and 1

    b. How texture coordinates are handled that are lower or higher than the range of 0 to 1

    c. How the texture color is rendered

Have a go hero – Using texture modes

Try using texture coordinates that are larger than 2 or are negative.

Scrolling a texture

We have seen several texture modes, but this is only one attribute a material file can have. Now, we are going to use another attribute that can also be quite useful.

Time for action – preparing to scroll a texture

This time, we are going to change our quad to see the effect of the new material:

1. Change the used material to `MyMaterial8` and also change the texture coordinates from 2 to 0.2:

```
manual->begin("MyMaterial8", RenderOperation::OT_TRIANGLE_LIST);
manual->position(5.0, 0.0, 0.0);
manual->textureCoord(0.0,0.2);
manual->position(-5.0, 10.0, 0.0);
manual->textureCoord(0.2,0.0);
manual->position(-5.0, 0.0, 0.0);
manual->textureCoord(0.2,0.2);
manual->position(5.0, 10.0, 0.0);
manual->textureCoord(0.0,0.0);
```

2. Now create the new material `MyMaterial8` in the material file. This time, we don't need any texture mode; just use the texture `terr_rock6.jpg`:

```
material MyMaterial8
{
    technique
    {
        pass
        {
            texture_unit
            {
                texture terr_rock6.jpg
            }
        }
    }
}
```

3. Compile and run the application. You should see a part of the stone texture that we had seen before.

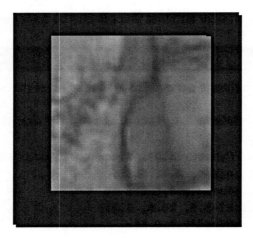

What just happened?

We are only seeing a part of the texture because our quad only has a texture coordinate that is going up to 0.2; this means four-fifths of the texture isn't rendered onto our quad. Everything that has happened in this Time for action should be easy to understand, as it's just a repetition of the stuff we learned in this chapter up until now. If necessary, read the chapter again.

Time for action – scrolling a texture

Now that we have prepared our quad, let's scroll the texture:

1. Add the following line into the texture block of the material to scroll the texture:

```
scroll 0.8 0.8
```

2. Compile and run the application. This time, you should see a different part of the texture.

What just happened?

The scroll attribute changes the texture coordinates with the given offset. The following is a diagram showing the effect of scrolling. The upper-right corner was the first part of the texture we rendered and the lower-left corner was the part of the texture we rendered with the scroll applied.

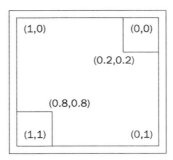

This attribute can be used to change the texture coordinates without the need for changing the UV coordinates of a model itself.

Animated scrolling

Being able to scroll the texture in the material isn't exactly breathtaking, but it can help to save some time in comparison to retexturing a complete model. Let's add a bit of dynamic scrolling.

Time for action – adding animated scrolling

We can also make the scrolling of the texture dynamic. Let's do it:

1. Create a new material and change the scroll attribute to animated scrolling:

   ```
   scroll_anim 0.01 0.01
   ```

2. Remember to also change the used material of the manual object; otherwise, you won't see any changes.

3. Compile and run the application. When you look carefully, you should see the texture moving from the upper-right to the lower-left corner. I can't show a picture of this because printing isn't yet able to show animations (maybe in the future).

What just happened?

We used another attribute to make the texture scroll. Besides the name, this attribute is almost similar to the scroll attribute, with the small, but important, difference that now the offset we set is per second.

There are many more attributes that we can use for manipulating a texture. A complete list can be found at `http://www.ogre3d.org/docs/manual/manual_17.html#SEC9`.

Inheriting materials

Before we touch more complex topics like shaders, we will try inheriting from materials.

Time for action – inheriting from a material

We will create two new materials and one new quad. We will also change how our quad is defined:

1. For this example, we need a quad that simply displays one texture. Change the quad definition to use only texture coordinates between 0 and 1 and remember to change the used material to `MyMaterial11`, which we will create soon:

```
manual->begin("MyMaterial11", RenderOperation::OT_TRIANGLE_LIST);
manual->position(5.0, 0.0, 0.0);
manual->textureCoord(0.0,1.0);
manual->position(-5.0, 10.0, 0.0);
manual->textureCoord(1.0,0.0);
manual->position(-5.0, 0.0, 0.0);
manual->textureCoord(1.0,1.0);
manual->position(5.0, 10.0, 0.0);
manual->textureCoord(0.0,0.0);

manual->index(0);
manual->index(1);
manual->index(2);
manual->index(0);
manual->index(3);
manual->index(1);
manual->end();
```

2. The new material will use the rock texture and use the attribute `rotate_anim`, which rotates the texture with the given speed. But the most important thing is to name the texture unit `texture1`:

```
material MyMaterial11
{
    technique
    {
        pass
        {
            texture_unit texture1
            {
             texture terr_rock6.jpg
             rotate_anim 0.1
            }
```

```
        }
      }
    }
```

3. Now create a second quad and translate it 15 units on the x-axis so that it doesn't intersect with the first quad. Also use the `setMaterialName()` function to change the material used by the entity to `MyMaterial12`:

```
ent = mSceneMgr->createEntity("Quad");
ent->setMaterialName("MyMaterial12");node = mSceneMgr-
>getRootSceneNode()->createChildSceneNode("Node2",Ogre::Vect
or3(15,0,0));
node->attachObject(ent);
```

4. The last thing to do is to create `MyMaterial12`. We will inherit from `MyMaterial11` and set the texture alias to another texture that we want to use:

```
material MyMaterial12 : MyMaterial11
{
   set_texture_alias texture1 Water02.jpg
}
```

5. Compile and run the application, and you should see two quads with rotating textures—one is a rock texture and the other one is a water texture.

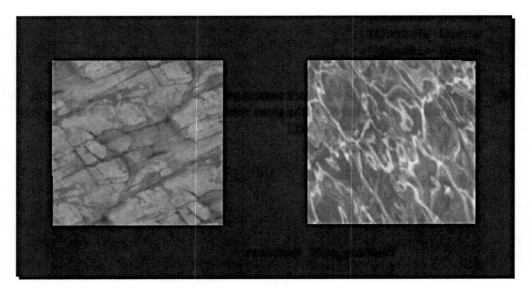

What just happened?

We created two quads, each with its own material. Steps 1 and 2 just modified the quad to only use texture coordinates in the range of [0,1]. In step 2, we created our material for the quad and used the new attribute `rotate_anim x`, which rotates the texture x turns per second—nothing fancy. Also we gave the texture unit the name `texture1`; we need this name later. In step 3, we created another instance of the quad and used the `setMaterialName()` function to change the material used by the entity. The important part was step 4. Here we created a new material by using inheritance, a concept which should be familiar. The syntax is the same as in C++, `NewName : ParentName`. In this case, `MyMaterial12` inherits from `MyMaterial11`. Then we use the attribute `set_texture_alias` that binds the texture `Water02.jpg` to the texture unit `texture1`. In this case, we replace `terr_rock6.jpg` with `Water02.jpg`. Because this is the only change we wanted to make with our new material, we can stop here.

The use of texture aliases enables us to create a lot of materials that only differ in the used texture without the need to write each material from the ground up, and we all know that duplication should always be avoided, if possible.

We have covered a lot of things about materials, but there is a lot more that we can do. We have covered the basics and with the help of the documentation, it should be possible to understand most of the other attributes that can be used in materials. Just take a look here `http://www.ogre3d.org/docs/manual/manual_14.html#SEC23`. We will now go a bit deeper and learn how to program our graphics card with the so-called shaders.

Fixed Function Pipeline and shaders

In this chapter, we have used the so-called Fixed Function Pipeline. This is the rendering pipeline on the graphics card that produces those nice shiny pictures we love looking at. As the prefix Fixed suggests, there isn't a lot of freedom to manipulate the Fixed Function Pipeline for the developer. We can tweak some parameters using the material files, but nothing fancy. That's where shaders can help fill the gap. **Shaders** are small programs that can be loaded onto the graphics card and then function as a part of the rendering process. These shaders can be thought of as little programs written in a C-like language with a small, but powerful, set of functions. With shaders, we can almost completely control how our scene is rendered and also add a lot of new effects that weren't possible with only the Fixed Function Pipeline.

Render Pipeline

To understand shaders, we need to first understand how the rendering process works as a whole. When rendering, each vertex of our model is translated from local space into camera space, then each triangle gets rasterized. This means, the graphics card calculates how to represent the model in an image. These image parts are called fragments. Each fragment is then processed and manipulated. We could apply a specific part of a texture to this fragment to texture our model or we could simply assign it a color when rendering a model in only one color. After this processing, the graphics card tests if the fragment is covered by another fragment that is nearer to the camera or if it is the fragment nearest to the camera. If this is true, the fragment gets displayed on the screen. In newer hardware, this step can occur before the processing of the fragment. This can save a lot of computation time if most of the fragments won't be seen in the end result. The following is a very simplified graph showing the pipeline:

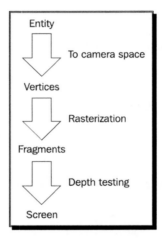

With almost each new graphics card generation, new shader types were introduced. It began with vertex and pixel/fragment shaders. The task of the vertex shader is to transform the vertices into camera space, and if needed, modify them in any way, like when doing animations completely on the GPU. The pixel/fragment shader gets the rasterized fragments and can apply a texture to them or manipulate them in other ways, for example, for lighting models with an accuracy of a pixel. There are also other shader stages, such as Geometry shaders, but we won't discuss them in this book because they are pretty new, not widely supported, and also are out of the scope of this book.

Time for action – our first shader application

Let's write our first vertex and fragment shaders:

1. In our application, we only need to change the used material. Change it to
   `MyMaterial13`. Also remove the second quad:

   ```
   manual->begin("MyMaterial13", RenderOperation::OT_TRIANGLE_LIST);
   ```

2. Now we need to create this material in our material file. First, we are going to define
   the fragment shader. Ogre 3D needs five pieces of information about the shader:

   - The name of the shader
   - In which language it is written
   - In which source file it is stored
   - How the main function of this shader is called
   - In what profile we want the shader to be compiled

3. All this information should be in the material file:

   ```
   fragment_program MyFragmentShader1 cg
   {
     source Ogre3DBeginnersGuideShaders.cg
     entry_point MyFragmentShader1
     profiles ps_1_1  arbfp1
   }
   ```

4. The vertex shader needs the same parameter, but we also have to define a
   parameter that is passed from Ogre 3D to our shader. This contains the matrix
   that we will use for transforming our quad into camera space:

   ```
   vertex_program MyVertexShader1 cg
    {
     source Ogre3DBeginnerGuideShaders.cg
     entry_point MyVertexShader1
     profiles vs_1_1 arbvp1

     default_params
     {
       param_named_auto worldViewMatrix worldviewproj_matrix
     }
   }
   ```

5. The material itself just uses the vertex and fragment shader names to reference them:

```
material MyMaterial13
{
    technique
    {
        pass
        {
      vertex_program_ref MyVertexShader1
            {
            }
            fragment_program_ref MyFragmentShader1
            {
            }
        }
    }
}
```

6. Now we need to write the shader itself. Create a file named `Ogre3DBeginnersGuideShaders.cg` in the `media\materials\programs` folder of your Ogre 3D SDK.

7. Each shader looks like a function. One difference is that we can use the `out` keyword to mark a parameter as an outgoing parameter instead of the default incoming parameter. The `out` parameters are used by the rendering pipeline for the next rendering step. The `out` parameters of a vertex shader are processed and then passed into the pixel shader as an `in` parameter. The `out` parameter from a pixel shader is used to create the final render result. Remember to use the correct name for the function; otherwise, Ogre 3D won't find it. Let's begin with the fragment shader because it's easier:

```
void MyFragmentShader1(out float4 color: COLOR)
```

8. The fragment shader will return the color blue for every pixel we render:

```
{
    color = float4(0,0,1,0);
}
```

9. That's all for the fragment shader; now we come to the vertex shader. The vertex shader has three parameters—the position for the vertex, the translated position of the vertex as an `out` variable, and as a uniform variable for the matrix we are using for the translation:

```
void MyVertexShader1(
        float4 position          : POSITION,
        out float4 oPosition     : POSITION,
        uniform float4x4 worldViewMatrix)
```

10. Inside the shader, we use the matrix and the incoming position to calculate the outgoing position:

```
{
    oPosition = mul(worldViewMatrix, position);
}
```

11. Compile and run the application. You should see our quad, this time rendered in blue.

What just happened?

Quite a lot happened here; we will start with step 2. Here we defined the fragment shader we are going to use. As discussed before, Ogre 3D needs five pieces of information for a shader. We define a fragment shader with the keyword `fragment_program`, followed by the name we want the fragment program to have, then a space, and at the end, the language in which the shader will be written. As for programs, shader code was written in assembly and in the early days, programmers had to write shader code in assembly because there wasn't another language to be used. But also, as with general programming language, soon there came high-level programming to ease the pain of writing shader code. At the moment, there are three different languages that shaders can be written in: HLSL, GLSL, and CG. The shader language HLSL is used by DirectX and GLSL is the language used by OpenGL. CG was developed by NVidia in cooperation with Microsoft and is the language we are going to use. This language is compiled during the start up of our application to their respective assembly code. So shaders written in HLSL can only be used with DirectX and GLSL shaders with OpenGL. But CG can compile to DirectX and OpenGL shader assembly code; that's the reason why we are using it to be truly cross platform. That's two of the five pieces of information that Ogre 3D needs. The other three are given in the curly brackets. The syntax is like a property file—first the key and then the value. One key we use is source followed by the file where the shader is stored. We don't need to give the full path, just the filename will do, because Ogre 3D scans our directories and only needs the filename to find the file.

Another key we are using is `entry_point` followed by the name of the function we are going to use for the shader. In the code file, we created a function called `MyFragmentShader1` and we are giving Ogre 3D this name as the entry point for our fragment shader. This means, each time we need the fragment shader, this function is called. The function has only one parameter `out float4 color : COLOR`. The prefix `out` signals that this parameter is an out parameter, meaning we will write a value into it, which will be used by the render pipeline later on. The type of this parameter is called `float4`, which simply is an array of four float values. For colors, we can think of it as a tuple (r,g,b,a) where r stands for red, g for green, b for blue, and a for alpha: the typical tuple to description colors. After the name of the parameter, we got a `: COLOR`. In CG, this is called a semantic describing for what the parameter is used in the context of the render pipeline. The parameter `:COLOR` tells the render pipeline that this is a color. In combination with the `out` keyword and the fact that this is a fragment shader, the render pipeline can deduce that this is the color we want our fragment to have.

The last piece of information we supply uses the keyword profiles with the values `ps_1_1` and `arbfp1`. To understand this, we need to talk a bit about the history of shaders. With each generation of graphics cards, a new generation of shaders have been introduced. What started as a fairly simple C-like programming language without even IF conditions are now really complex and powerful programming languages. Right now, there are several different versions for shaders and each with a unique function set. Ogre 3D needs to know which of these versions we want to use. `ps_1_1` means pixel shader version 1.1 and `arbfp1` means fragment program version 1. We need both profiles because `ps_1_1` is a DirectX specific function set and `arbfp1` is a function subset for OpenGL. We say we are cross platform, but sometimes we need to define values for both platforms. All subsets can be found at `http://www.ogre3d.org/docs/manual/manual_18.html`. That's all needed to define the fragment shader in our material file. In step 3, we defined our vertex shader. This part is very similar to the fragment shader definition code; the main difference is the `default_params` block. This block defines parameters that are given to the shader during runtime. `param_named_auto` defines a parameter that is automatically passed to the shader by Ogre 3D. After this key, we need to give the parameter a name and after this, the value keyword we want it to have. We name the parameter `worldViewMatrix`; any other name would also work, and the value we want it to have has the key `worldviewproj_matrix`. This key tells Ogre 3D we want our parameter to have the value of the `WorldViewProjection` matrix. This matrix is used for transforming vertices from local into camera space. A list of all keyword values can be found at `http://www.ogre3d.org/docs/manual/manual_23.html#SEC128`. How we use these values will be seen shortly.

Step 4 used the work we did before. As always, we defined our material with one technique and one pass; we didn't define a texture unit but used the keyword `vertex_program_ref`. After this keyword, we need to put the name of a vertex program we defined, in our case, this is `MyVertexShader1`. If we wanted, we could have put some more parameters into the definition, but we didn't need to, so we just opened and closed the block with curly brackets. The same is true for `fragment_program_ref`.

Writing a shader

Now that we have defined all necessary things in our material file, let's write the shader code itself. Step 6 defines the function head with the parameter we discussed before, so we won't go deeper here. Step 7 defines the function body; for this fragment shader, the body is extremely simple. We created a new float4 tuple (0,0,1,0), describes the color blue and assigns this color to our `out` parameter color. The effect is that everything that is rendered with this material will be blue. There isn't more to the fragment shader, so let's move on to the vertex shader. Step 8 defines the function header. The vertex shader has 3 parameters— two are marked as positions using CG semantics and the other parameter is a 4x4 matrix using float4 as values named `worldViewMatrix`. Before the parameter type definition, there is the keyword `uniform`.

Each time our vertex shader is called, it gets a new vertex as the position parameter input, calculates the position of this new vertex, and saves it in the `oPosition` parameter. This means with each call, the parameter changes. This isn't true for the `worldViewMatrix`. The keyword `uniform` denotes parameters that are constant over one draw call. When we render our quad, the `worldViewMatrix` doesn't change while the rest of the parameters are different for each vertex processed by our vertex shader. Of course, in the next frame, the `worldViewMatrix` will probably have changed. Step 9 creates the body of the vertex shader. In the body, we multiply the vertex that we got with the world matrix to get the vertex translated into camera space. This translated vertex is saved in the `out` parameter to be processed by the rendering pipeline. We will look more closely into the render pipeline after we have experimented with shaders a bit more.

Texturing with shaders

We have painted our quad in blue, but we would like to use the previous texture.

Time for action – using textures in shaders

1. Create a new material named `MyMaterial14`. Also create two new shaders named `MyFragmentShader2` and `MyVertexShader2`. Remember to copy the fragment and vertex program definitions in the material file. Add to the material file a texture unit with the rock texture:

    ```
    texture_unit
    {
      texture terr_rock6.jpg
    }
    ```

2. We need to add two new parameters to our fragment shader. The first is a two tuple of floats for the texture coordinates. Therefore, we also use the semantic to mark the parameter as the first texture coordinates we are using. The other new parameter is of type `sampler2D`, which is another name for texture. Because the texture doesn't change on a per fragment basis, we mark it as `uniform`. This keyword indicates that the parameter value comes from outside the CG program and is set by the rendering environment, in our case, by Ogre 3D:

    ```
    void MyFragmentShader2(float2 uv      : TEXCOORD0,
                  out float4 color : COLOR,
                  uniform sampler2D texture)
    ```

3. In the fragment shader, replace the color assignment with the following line:

    ```
    color = tex2D(texture, uv);
    ```

4. The vertex shader also needs some new parameters—one `float2` for the incoming texture coordinates and one `float2` as the outgoing texture coordinates. Both are our `TEXCOORD0` because one is the incoming and the other is the outgoing `TEXCOORD0`:

```
void MyVertexShader2(
        float4 position          : POSITION,
        out float4 oPosition     : POSITION,
        float2 uv        : TEXCOORD0,
        out float2 oUv           : TEXCOORD0,
        uniform float4x4 worldViewMatrix)
```

5. In the body, we calculate the outgoing position of the vertex:

```
oPosition = mul(worldViewMatrix, position);
```

6. For the texture coordinates, we assign the incoming value to the outgoing value:

```
oUv = uv;
```

7. Remember to change the used material in the application code, and then compile and run it. You should see the quad with the rock texture.

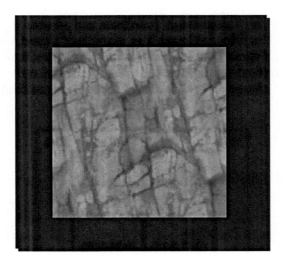

What just happened?

Step 1 just added a texture unit with the rock texture, nothing fancy. Step 2 added a `float2` for saving the texture coordinates; also we are using `sampler2D` for the first time. `sampler2D` is just the name for a two-dimensional texture lookup function, and because it doesn't change per fragment and comes from outside the CG program, we declared it uniform. Step 3 used the `tex2D` function, which takes a `sampler2D` and `float2` as the input parameter and returns a color as `float4`. This function uses the `float2` as the position to retrieve a color from the `sampler2D` object and returns this color. Basically, it's just a lookup in the texture for the given coordinates. Step 4 added two texture coordinates to the vertex shader—one as incoming and one as outgoing. Step 5 assigned the incoming to the outgoing parameter. The magic happens in the render pipeline.

What happens in the render pipeline?

Our vertex shader gets each vertex and transforms it into camera space. After all vertices have gone through this transformation, the render pipeline sees which vertices form a triangle and then rasterizes them. In this process, the triangles get split into fragments. Each fragment is a candidate for becoming pixels on the screen. It will become pixels if it's not covered by another fragment and therefore can't be seen. During this process, the render pipeline interpolates the vertex data like texture coordinates over each fragment. After this process, each fragment has its own texture coordinate and we used this to look up the color value from the texture. The following image is an example of a quad, which is represented by four fragments. Each fragment has its own texture coordinates. It also shows how we can imagine the texture coordinates, related to the pixels. In the real world, this depends on the render pipeline and can change, but this is a helpful model we can think with, even if it's not 100 percent accurate.

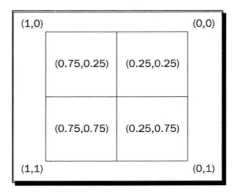

The same interpolation is used when we assign each vertex a color. Let's investigate this effect a bit more.

Have a go hero – combining color and texture coordinates

Create a new vertex and fragment shader called `MyVertexShader3` and
`MyFragmentShader3` respectively. The fragment shader should render everything in green
and the vertex shader should calculate the position of the vertex in camera space and
simply pass the texture coordinates to the fragment shader. The fragment shader doesn't do
anything with them yet, but we will need them later.

Interpolating color values

To see the effect of interpolation better, let's replace the texture with colors.

Time for action – using colors to see interpolation

To see how color interpolation works we need to change our code a bit.

1. Again, copy the material and make sure to adjust all names.

2. The only thing we need to change in the material is that we don't need a texture
unit. We can just delete it.

3. In the application code, we need to replace the `textureCoord()` with `color()`:

```
manual->position(5.0,  0.0,  0.0);
manual->color(0,0,1);
manual->position(-5.0,  10.0,  0.0);
manual->color(0,1,0);
manual->position(-5.0,  0.0,  0.0);
manual->color(0,1,0);
manual->position(5.0,  10.0,  0.0);
manual->color(0,0,1);
```

4. The vertex shader also needs some adjustments. Replace the two texture coordinate
parameters with color parameters and also change the assignment line:

```
void MyVertexShader4(
        float4 position       : POSITION,
        out float4 oPosition    : POSITION,
    float4 color      :COLOR,
    out float4 ocolor     :COLOR,
        uniform float4x4 worldViewMatrix)
{
    oPosition = mul(worldViewMatrix, position);
  ocolor = color;
}
```

5. The fragment shader now has two color parameters—one incoming and one outgoing:

```
void MyFragmentShader4(  float4 color : COLOR,
                out float4 oColor : COLOR)

{
    oColor = color;
}
```

6. Compile and run the application. You should see the quad with the right side blue and the left side green and the colors should fade into each other in between.

What just happened?

In step 3, we saw another function of the manual object, namely, adding color to a vertex using three float values for red, green, and blue. Step 4 replaced the texture coordinates with color parameters—this time we wanted colors not textures. The same is true for step 5. This example wasn't really difficult or exciting, but it shows how interpolation works. This gives us a better understanding of how the vertex and fragment shader also work together.

Replacing the quad with a model

The quad, as an object for experimentation, gets a bit boring, so let's replace it with the Sinbad model.

Time for action – replacing the quad with a model

Using the previous code we will now use Sinbad instead of a quad.

1. Delete all the code for the quad; just leave the scene node creation code in place.

2. Create an instance of `Sinbad.mesh`, attach it to the scene node, and use the `MaterialManager` to set the material of the entity to `MyMaterial14`:

```
void createScene()
{
   Ogre::SceneNode* node = mSceneMgr->getRootSceneNode()-
>createChildSceneNode("Node1");
   Ogre::Entity* ent = mSceneMgr->createEntity("Entity1","Sinbad.
mesh");
   ent->setMaterialName("MyMaterial14");
   node->attachObject(ent);
}
```

3. Compile and run the application; because `MyMaterial14` uses the rock texture, Sinbad will be made out of rock.

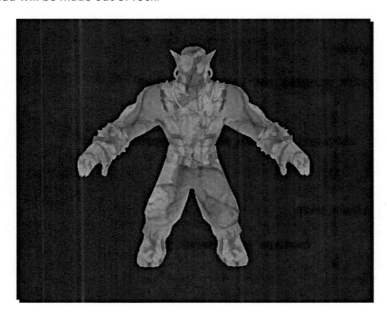

What just happened?

Everything that has happened here should be familiar to you. We created an instance of a model, attached it to a scene node, and changed the material to MyMaterial14.

Making the model pulse on the x-axis

Up until now, we only worked with the fragment shader. Now it's time for the vertex shader.

Time for action – adding a pulse

Adding a pulse to our model is quite easy and only needs some changes to our code.

1. This time, we only need a new vertex shader because we are going to use the existing fragment shader. Create a new vertex shader named MyVertexShader5 and use it in the new material MyMaterial17, but use MyFragmentShader2 because this shader only textures our model and nothing more:

```
material MyMaterial17
{
  technique
  {
      pass
      {
    vertex_program_ref MyVertexShader5
          {
          }

        fragment_program_ref MyFragmentShader2
          {
          }


    texture_unit
          {
              texture terr_rock6.jpg
          }
      }
  }
}
```

2. The new vertex shader is the same as the ones we've seen before; just add a new parameter in the `default_params` block called `pulseTime` that gets the value from the `time` keyword:

```
vertex_program MyVertexShader5 cg
  {
    source Ogre3DBeginnerGuideShaders.cg
    entry_point MyVertexShader5
    profiles vs_1_1 arbvp1

    default_params
    {
      param_named_auto worldViewMatrix worldviewproj_matrix
      param_named_auto pulseTime time
    }
  }
```

3. We don't need to change anything in the application itself. The only thing left to do is to create the new vertex shader. `MyVertexShader5` is based on `MyVertexShader3`. Just add a new line that multiplies the x value of the `oPosition` variable with (`2+sin(pulseTime)`):

```
void MyVertexShader5( uniform float pulseTime,
          float4 position      : POSITION,
          out float4 oPosition  : POSITION,
       float2 uv       : TEXCOORD0,
       out float2 oUv        : TEXCOORD0,
          uniform float4x4 worldViewMatrix)
{
    oPosition = mul(worldViewMatrix, position);
  oPosition.x *= (2+sin(pulseTime));
  oUv = uv;

}
```

4. Compile and run the application. You should see Sinbad pulsing on the x-axis between his normal width and the threefold of his width.

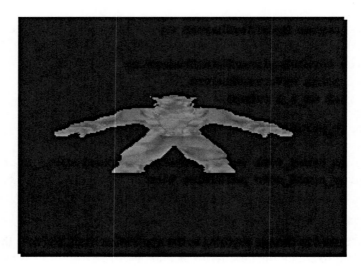

What just happened?

We made the model pulse on the x-axis. We needed a second parameter for the vertex shader, which contains the current time. We used the sine of the time with two added to get a value between 1 and 3, with which we multiplied the x part of each translated vertex of the model. In action, this changes the position of each single vertex in each frame a bit, creating the effect of pulsing. Using this technique, we can practically pass any data into a shader to modify its behavior. This is the basis for a lot of effects used in games.

Summary

We learned a lot in this chapter about materials and Ogre 3D.

Specifically, we covered:

- How to create new materials
- How to apply textures to an entity using a material
- How to create shaders and refer to them in materials
- How the render pipeline works and how to modify the geometry of models using the vertex shader

In the next chapter, we are going to create post-processing effects to improve the visual quality of our scene or create completely new visual styles.

8
The Compositor Framework

In this chapter, we are going to add post processing effects to scenes, which can improve their visual quality and make them look more interesting. This chapter will show you how to create compositors and how to combine them to create new effects.

In this chapter, we will:

- ◆ Create compositor scripts and apply them to our scene
- ◆ Work with viewports to create split screens
- ◆ Use user input to manipulate shader parameters, which are used by compositors

So let's get on with it...

Preparing a scene

We are going to use compositor effects. However, before using them, we are going to prepare a scene that will be used to show the different effects we can create.

Time for action – preparing the scene

We are going to use the last example from the previous chapter:

1. Remove the line that changes the material of the model. We want it to use its original material:

```
ent->setMaterial(Ogre::MaterialManager::getSingleton().
getByName("MyMaterial18"));
```

2. The application class should now look like this:

```
class Example69 : public ExampleApplication
{
private:

public:

    void createScene()
    {
        Ogre::SceneNode* node = mSceneMgr-
>getRootSceneNode()->createChildSceneNode("Node1",Ogre::Vect
or3(0,0,450));
        Ogre::Entity* ent = mSceneMgr-
>createEntity("Entity1","Sinbad.mesh");
        node->attachObject(ent);
    }
};
```

3. Compile and run the application. You should see an instance of Sinbad rendered with its normal material.

What just happened?

We created a simple scene on which we will now use a compositor effect.

Adding the first compositor

Before explaining what a compositor is, let's use one and then discuss the technical details.

Time for action – adding a compositor

This is going to be our first compositor. We will use the scene and prepare to see its effect.

1. We need a new material for this, which does nothing at the moment. Add this new material in the material file that we previously used and name it `Ogre3DBeginnersGuide/Comp1`:

    ```
    material Ogre3DBeginnersGuide/Comp1
    {
         technique
        {
          pass
          {
                    texture_unit
              {
              }
          }
        }
    }
    ```

2. Next, create a new file for storing our compositor scripts. In the same directory as the material file, create a file named `Ogre3DBeginnersGuide.compositor`.

3. In this file, define our compositor using the same scheme as we did for materials:

    ```
    compositor Compositor1
    {
      technique
        {
    ```

4. Next, define a target where our scene is rendered to before we can modify it:

    ```
    texture scene target_width target_height PF_R8G8B8
    ```

5. Define the content of our target. In this case, it's the scene that was rendered before:

```
target scene
        {
                input previous
        }
```

6. The last step in the compositor script is to define the output:

```
target_output
            {
```

7. The compositor doesn't need any input and renders its result to a quad that covers the whole screen. This quad uses the material Ogre3DBeginnersGuide/Comp1 and needs our scene target as a texture input:

```
input none
pass render_quad
{
material Ogre3DBeginnersGuide/Comp1
input 0 scene
}
```

8. That's all for this compositor. Close all open curly brackets:

```
            }
        }
}
```

9. Now that we have a finished a compositor script, let's add it to our scene. For this, we use CompositorManager and the viewport of our camera. Add the code to the createScene() function:

```
Ogre::CompositorManager::getSingleton().addCompositor(mCamera->getViewport(), "Compositor1");
Ogre::CompositorManager::getSingleton().
setCompositorEnabled(mCamera->getViewport(), "Compositor1", true);
```

10. Compile and run the application, and you should see the same scene as before.

What just happened?

We added our first compositor using a compositor file containing our compositor script. Step 1 just created an empty material, which simply rendered everything it got without any added effects. Step 2 created a new file to store our compositor scripts; it's like material files just for compositors. Step 3 is also pretty familiar: we named our first compositor `Compositor1` and defined a technique to use just like materials compositors have different techniques for different target graphic cards. The interesting part starts with step 4: here we created a new texture named scene which has the same dimensions as the target texture we are rendering to, and this texture used eight bits for each color part. This is defined by `PF_R8G8B8`.

How the compositor works

But why do we need to create a new texture in the first place? To understand this, we need to understand how a compositor works. Compositors modify the appearance of a scene after it has been rendered. It's like post processing in movies where they add all the computer effects after the shooting of a movie. To be able to do this, the compositor needs the rendered scene as a texture, so it can be modified further. We created this texture in step 4, and in step 5, we told Ogre 3D to fill this texture with the scene we rendered before. This was done with `input previous`. Now we have a texture that contains our scene rendered, the next thing our compositor needs to do is create a new image, which is displayed on the monitor. This is done in step 6 using the keyword `output` in combination with a target block. Step 7 defines this output. We don't need any input because we already have our scene in the scene texture. To render the modified texture, we need a quad that covers the whole monitor, onto which we can render the texture with the modified scene. This is achieved with the `pass` keyword followed by the `render_quad` identifier. There are several other identifiers we can use in combination with the `pass` keyword. They can be found in the documentation (http://www.ogre3d.org/docs/manual/manual_32.html#SEC163). Inside the pass block, we define several attributes we want to use for this rendering pass. This is the first material we want the quad to use; here we just use the material we defined beforehand, which renders the texture we are giving it to the quad without modifying it. The next attribute defines additional input like textures; here we say the first texture we want as input should be the scene texture. In fact, this means we want our scene rendered to a texture and applied to a quad that covers the whole screen. With this, we won't see any difference between the rendered scene with or without a compositor. This will change when we add some code to our material, which modifies the incoming texture to add additional effects.

Step 9 adds the compositor to our viewport and then enables it; we add compositors to a viewport and not to our scene because compositors modify the appearance of a scene seen through a camera, and what a camera sees is defined within the viewport. So if we want to modify the appearance of a complete scene, we would add the compositor to the object that defines the appearance of the scene itself.

The following is a simplified diagram showing the workflow of our compositor and an abridged version of the compositor script, which is the code for the step shown by the diagram.

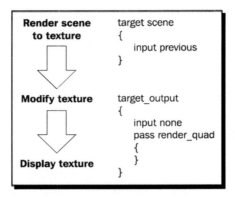

Modifying the texture

We have rendered our scene to a texture and displayed it without modifying it. This is rather pointless, so let's spice it up.

Time for action – modifying the texture

We will use a fragment shader to modify the texture, so change the material to also make use of a fragment shader. Also copy the material and the compositor. This compositor should have the name `Compositor2`, the material `Ogre3DBeginnersGuide/Comp2`.

1. fragment_program_ref MyFragmentShader5

    ```
    {
    }
    ```

2. Don't forget to define the fragment program in the material file before using the reference:

    ```
    fragment_program MyFragmentShader5 cg
    {
         source Ogre3DBeginnersGuideShaders.cg
      entry_point MyFragmentShader5
    ```

```
        profiles ps_1_1   arbfp1
    }
```

3. Also create a new fragment shader in our shader file. This shader has, as input, the texture coordinates and a texture sample. Once the color of the fragment is computed, this color is returned:

```
void MyFragmentShader5(float2 uv : TEXCOORD0,
                                out float4 color : COLOR,
                                uniform sampler2D texture)
    {
```

4. Get the color of the texture at the position of the texture coordinates:

```
float4 temp_color = tex2D(texture, uv);
```

5. Convert the color to grayscale:

```
float greyvalue = temp_color.r * 0.3 + temp_color.g * 0.59 + temp_
color.b * 0.11;
```

6. And use this value as all three values of the output color:

```
color = float4(greyvalue,greyvalue,greyvalue,0);
```

7. Compile and run the application. You should see the same model, but this time in grayscale:

What just happened?

We added a fragment shader to our compositor. After rendering our scene, the full screen quad got rendered with the scene texture using our fragment shader. The fragment shader queries the texture for the color it has at its position using its texture coordinates. Then it converts the RGB color into a grayscale color by simply adding the three-color channel multiplied with a factor. For red, the factor is 0.3, for green 0.59, and for blue 0.11. These values represent how much each color contributes to the brightness reception of the human eye. Adding the color values using these factors creates a pretty good approximation for the black and white values. After this first compositor effect, we are going to create a new one that doesn't convert the picture to black and white, but rather inverts the colors.

Inverting the image

Now it's time to create a color-inverted version of our scene using another compositor.

Time for action – inverting the image

Using the code from the black and white compositor, we are now going to invert our image.

1. Copy the shader, the material, and the compositor because later we will need both—the black and white compositor and this one. Then change the fragment shader of this copy. The new fragment shader should have the name MyFragmentShader6, the material Ogre3DBeginnersGuide/Comp3, and the compositor Compositor3.

2. This time, get the color value of the texture at the position of the fragment and then subtract each single value from 1.0 to get the inverted value:

   ```
   color = float4( 1.0 - temp_color.r,1.0 - temp_color.g, 1.0 - temp_
   color.b,0);
   ```

3. Compile and run the application. This time, the background should be white and Sinbad should be in some pretty strange colors as shown in the following image:

What just happened?

We changed our fragment shader to invert the color values instead of converting them to black and white. The rest of the application hasn't changed. Converting RGB color values is really easy: just subtract each individual value from its maximum value, in our case, 1.0. The resulting color is the inverted version of the original color.

Combining compositors

This is getting boring rather quickly, so let's try combining two compositor effects.

Time for action – combining two compositor effects

To combine two compositors, we need to create a new one:

1. To create a new compositor, we need two textures—one for storing the scene and one for storing some temporary results:

```
compositor Compositor4
{
    technique
    {
        texture scene target_width target_height PF_R8G8B8
            texture temp target_width target_height PF_R8G8B8
```

2. Fill the scene texture, as done previously, and then fill the temp texture using the scene texture and our black and white material:

```
target scene
    {
        input previous
    }

      target temp
    {
      pass render_quad
    {
      material Ogre3DBeginnersGuide/Comp2
      input 0 scene
      }
    }
```

3. Then use the temporary material and our invert material to create the output texture:

```
target_output
      {
          input none
          pass render_quad
          {
              material Ogre3DBeginnersGuide/Comp3
              input 0 temp
          }
      }
    }
}
```

4. Compile and run the application; you should see a scene that first got converted to black and white and was then inverted.

What just happened?

We created a second auxiliary texture; this texture was used as the render target for the black and white material, and then this texture with the black and white image of our scene was used as an input for the invert material, which then got rendered to the display.

Decreasing the texture count

In the previous section, we used two textures—one for the original scene and one for storing the intermediate result after the first of two steps have been done. Now let's try to only use one texture.

Time for action – decreasing the texture count

By using the previous code we are going to reduce the texture count of our compositor.

1. We need a new compositor, this time with only one texture:

```
compositor Compositor5
{
    technique
    {
        texture scene target_width target_height PF_R8G8B8
```

2. Then fill the texture with the rendered scene:

```
target scene
{
    input previous
}
```

3. Use this texture as the input texture as well as the output texture:

```
target scene
{
        pass render_quad
        {
                material Ogre3DBeginnersGuide/Comp2
                input 0 scene
        }
}
```

4. Again, use this texture as input for the final rendering:

```
target_output
{
        input none
        pass render_quad
        {
                material Ogre3DBeginnersGuide/Comp3
                input 0 scene
        }
}
```

5. Add the missing parenthesis:

```
}
}
```

6. Compile and run the application. The result will be the same, but this time we only use one texture.

What just happened?

We changed our compositor to only use one texture and discovered that we can use a texture more than once in a compositor. We also found out that we can use it as input and output texture at the same time.

Combining compositors in code

In the last two examples, we have seen how we can create more complex compositors by combining several render steps with different materials. We had to write a new compositor script to combine several render steps, even though we already had two compositors, each one describing one half of the final effect. Wouldn't it be nice to combine these two compositors to create the final effect without the need to write a new compositor script each time we want to combine some compositors? This is exactly what we are going to accomplish in the next example: making use of the compositor chain.

Time for action – combing two compositors in code

This time we don't need a new compositor. We are just going to modify the application a bit:

1. First add and enable the invert compositor:

   ```
   Ogre::CompositorManager::getSingleton().addCompositor(mCamera-
   >getViewport(), "Compositor3");
   Ogre::CompositorManager::getSingleton().
   setCompositorEnabled(mCamera->getViewport(), "Compositor3", true);
   ```

2. Then add the black and white compositor:

   ```
   Ogre::CompositorManager::getSingleton().addCompositor(mCamera-
   >getViewport(), "Compositor2");
   Ogre::CompositorManager::getSingleton().
   setCompositorEnabled(mCamera->getViewport(), "Compositor2", true);
   ```

3. Again compile and run the application. The result should be the same, only this time we combined the compositor in our application code rather than in the script itself.

What just happened?

We combined two compositors using the `addCompositor()` function. This function can take any number of compositors and chain them together; the output result of one will be the input of the other. If we want to add a compositor at a certain position, we can pass the position as the third parameter of the `addCompositor()` function. With this function, we can combine all sorts of different compositors without the need to write a single line of script. It also enables us to reuse compositors in other chains because we don't have to hardcode chains in scripts.

Have a go hero – swapping the green and blue color channels

Create a compositor that swaps the green and blue color channels of the scene. The result should look like the following image:

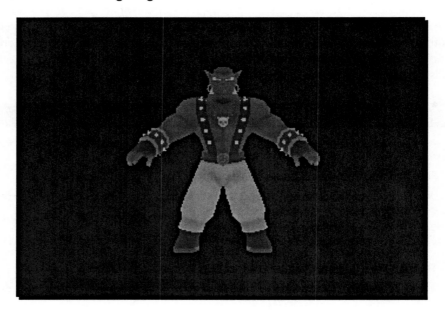

Something more complex

Until now, we have only seen pretty simple compositors. Let's make a complex one.

Time for action – complex compositor

We need a new compositor, material, and fragment shader:

1. The compositor script itself is nothing special. We need one texture for the scene and then directly use this texture as input for the output, which uses one material:

```
compositor Compositor7
{
    technique
    {
        texture scene target_width target_height PF_R8G8B8

        target scene
        {
```

```
                input previous
        }

        target_output
        {
            input none
            pass render_quad
            {
                material Ogre3DBeginnersGuide/Comp5
                input 0 scene
            }
        }
    }
}
```

2. The material itself is also nothing new; just add a fragment shader like always:

```
material Ogre3DBeginnersGuide/Comp5
{
    technique
    {
      pass
      {
                    fragment_program_ref MyFragmentShader8
            {
            }

                    texture_unit
            {
            }
      }
    }
}
```

3. Don't forget to add the definition of the fragment shader before using it in the material:

```
fragment_program MyFragmentShader8 cg
{
    source Ogre3DBeginnersGuideShaders.cg
    entry_point MyFragmentShader8
    profiles ps_1_1  arbfp1
}
```

4. Now to the interesting part. In the fragment shader, the header hasn't changed since the last time; only the code inside it has. First, we need two variables, namely, num and stepsize. The variable stepsize is one divided by num:

```
float num= 50;
float stepsize = 1.0/ num;
```

5. Then use both these variables and the texture coordinates to calculate the new texture coordinates:

```
float2 fragment = float2(stepsize * floor(uv.x * num),stepsize * floor(uv.y * num));
```

6. Use the new texture coordinates for retrieving the color from the texture:

```
color = tex2D(texture, fragment);
```

7. Change the program to use only this compositor and not the combined compositors anymore. Then compile and run the application. You should see some pixels of different colors instead of the normal instance of Sinbad.

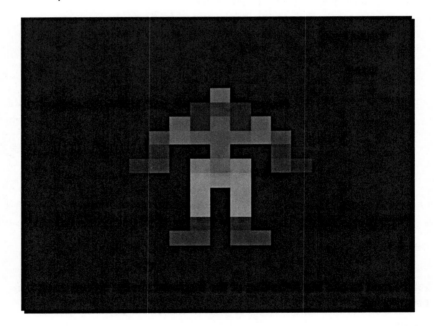

What just happened?

We created another compositor that really changed the appearance of our scene. It's almost unrecognizable. Step 1 and 2 are known and shouldn't be any challenge to understand. Step 3 sets to values we needed later. One is the number of pixels we want our dimensions to have, so we set this value to 50. This means each axis, x and y, will have 50 pixels. The second value was stepsize, which is 1 divided by the number of pixels. We need this value to calculate the texture coordinates.

In step 4, we calculated our new texture coordinates using the old ones and our two values we defined before. So how did we reduce the number of pixels using the fragment shader? Let's say our display resolution would be 100 X 100 pixels. If we render our scene in this resolution, the scene would look normal and we couldn't see the single pixel like we did in our previous example. To get this effect of using fewer pixels as the display, we need several neighbor pixels to have the same color. We do this in step 4 using simple math. The first step is to multiply the original texture coordinates with the number of pixels we want to have at the end and then the next step is to round this floating point number to the lower integer value. This will give us the number of the final pixel this pixel belongs to.

Let's say we have a scene with 4x4 resolution and we want the final image to have only 2x2. If we have the original texture coordinates (0.1,0.1), we multiply them with destination resolution and get (0.2,0.2). Then we round each of these values to the lower integer, which results in (0,0). This tells us that this pixel is in the final pixel (0,0). If the pixel has the coordinates (0.75,0.75), this would result in (1.5,1.5) and rounded in (1,1). With this simple operation, we can calculate to which final pixel each original pixel belongs.

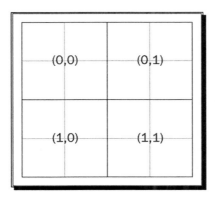

After we know to which final pixel each original pixel belongs, we need to calculate the texture coordinates to retrieve the color value from the original scene texture. For this, we need our second value called stepsize. The stepsize for our example is 0.5 because we divide 1 by the number of pixels we want, in this case 2. We then multiply the different texture coordinates with the stepsize to get the final texture coordinates.

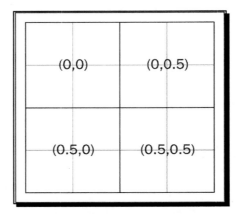

Using these values, we retrieve the color values from the scene texture and use the values as new color values. We can do this because four pixels have the same texture coordinate as the same color value, and therefore can be seen as one pixel. This is the magic to making a scene seem to have less pixels than it actually has. Of course, this technique isn't perfect. A much better approach would be to calculate the average overall original pixels that contribute to the final pixel.

Changing the number of pixels

We now have a compositor that can make our scene look like it has a lot less pixels than it actually does, but the number of pixels is hardcoded inside the fragment shader. When we want to use the compositor with a different number of pixels, we need to create a new compositor, material, and fragment shader, which isn't really efficient. The first step we will carry out is to define the number of pixels in the material and not in the fragment shader. This way, we can at least reuse the pixel shader for a different number of pixels we want the complete image to have.

Time for action – putting the number of pixels in the material

Now, we are going to control the number of pixels from our material rather than the shader itself.

1. Create a new fragment shader that has all the old parameters, a new one, which is uniform, and a float value named `numpixels`.

```
void MyFragmentShader9(float2 uv : TEXCOORD0,
                               out float4 color : COLOR,
                               uniform sampler2D texture,
                               uniform float numpixels)
{
```

2. Then, inside the fragment shader, use the new parameter to set the `num` variable:

```
float num = numpixels;
```

3. The rest of the shader is the same as the fragment shader before:

```
float stepsize = 1.0/num;

float2 fragment = float2(stepsize * floor(uv.x * num),stepsize *
floor(uv.y * num));
        color = tex2D(texture, fragment);
}
```

4. The material is a copy, which is almost the same as the original. Only the fragment program declaration needs to be changed a bit; or to be more precise, something new needs to be added such as a default `param` block. In this block, define the named parameter `numpixels`, which should be a float and has the value 500:

```
fragment_program MyFragmentShader9 cg
{
        source Ogre3DBeginnerGuideShaders.cg
        entry_point MyFragmentShader9
        profiles ps_1_1  arbfp1

        default_params
        {
                param_named numpixels float 500
        }
}
```

5. Now create a new compositor, which uses the new material, and change the program code to use the new compositor. Later, compile and run the application. You should see an instance of Sinbad being rendered, as there was less resolution than the usually well-defined meshes.

6. Now change the value of the `numpixels` to 25 and run the application again. There's no need to recompile because we just changed a script and not the code file.

What just happened?

We moved the definition of the number of pixels we wanted from the fragment shader to the material, allowing us to change the number without the need to change or duplicate the fragment shader.

To get there wasn't that complicated; we just needed to add a new uniform variable to the fragment shader and add a `default_params` block to the material, in which we declared the variable name and the type and value using the `param_named` keyword. For Ogre 3D to be able to map the parameter in the material and the parameter in the fragment shader, it is necessary that the type and name are the same.

Have a go hero – trying different numbers of pixels

Also run the application with the values 50, 100, and 1000 for `numpixels`.

Setting the variable in code

We have moved the `numpixels` variable from the fragment shader into the material script code. Now, let's try to set the value from the application code itself.

Time for action – setting the variable from the application

We can use the compositor, material, and fragment shader from the last example. Only the application itself must be modified:

1. We can't directly interact with the material of the quad that is rendered because our application doesn't know about the quad. The only way to interact with a compositor rendering process is through listeners. Ogre 3D provided an interface for the compositor listener. We can use this to create a new listener:

   ```
   class CompositorListener1 : public Ogre::CompositorInstance::Liste
   ner
   {
   public:
   ```

2. Override this method, which is called when the material is set up:

   ```
   void notifyMaterialSetup (uint32 pass_id, MaterialPtr &mat)
   {
   ```

3. Use the given pointer to the material to change the `numpixels` parameter to 125:

```
        mat->getBestTechnique()->getPass(pass_id)-
>getFragmentProgramParameters()->setNamedConstant("numpixels",125.
0f);
}
```

4. Add the following code to get the compositor instance after the code we added to enable the compositor in the `createScene()` function:

```
Ogre::CompositorInstance* comp =  Ogre::CompositorManager:
:getSingleton().getCompositorChain(mCamera->getViewport())-
>getCompositor("Compositor8");
```

5. We need a private variable to store the listener instance later on:

```
private:
        CompositorListener1* compListener;
```

6. When the application is created, we want the pointer to be `NULL`:

```
Example78()
{
        compListener = NULL;
}
```

7. What we create, we also need to destroy. Add a destructor to the application, which destroys the listener instance:

```
~Example78()
        {
                delete compListener;
        }
```

8. Now create the listener and add it to the compositor instance:

```
compListener = new CompositorListener1();
comp->addListener(compListener);
```

9. Compile and run the application. You should see a scene with some pixels, as shown in the following image:

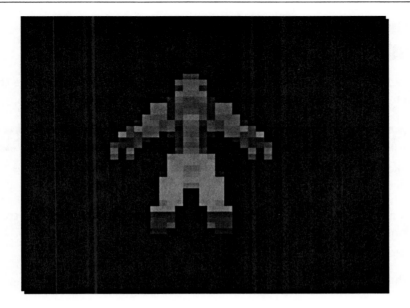

What just happened?

We changed our application to be able to set the number of pixels from the application code rather than the material script. Because compositors create materials and render passes, we don't have direct access to the quads that we use for rendering during runtime, which we need to change properties of materials like the fragment shader attributes. In order to still be able to access them, Ogre 3D offers a listener interface from which we inherited our own listener. This listener then overrode a method that is called when the material of the quad is generated. The function gets the ID of the pass it generated and a pointer to the material itself.

With the material pointer, we could select the technique that was going to be used, and using this technique, we got the pass and with it the parameter of the fragment shader. Once we had the parameter, we could change the number of pixels. This is a rather long call list because the parameter we wanted is deep down in the class hierarchy. As a side note, we can define parameters and change them in the application with normal materials like the compositor; we don't even need a listener, because when using entities we can get the material of an entity directly.

Changing the number of pixels while running the application

We can already change the number of pixels in the application code; let's go one step further and make it possible to change the number of pixels using user input.

Time for action – modifying the number of pixels with user input

We are going to use the knowledge about user input and frame listeners that we have seen in *Chapter 3, Camera, Light, and Shadow*:

1. Our application needs `FrameListener`. Add a new private variable to store the pointer to the application:

```
Ogre::FrameListener* FrameListener;
```

2. In the same way, `FrameListener` should also be inited with NULL:

```
Example79()
{
        FrameListener = NULL;
        compListener = NULL;
}
```

3. And it should be destroyed in the same way:

```
~Example79()
{
        if(compListener)
        {
                delete compListener;
        }
        if(FrameListener)
        {
                delete FrameListener;
        }
}
```

4. Lets add it and then implement it. The rest of the application class doesn't change:

```
void createFrameListener()
{
        FrameListener = new Example79FrameListener(mWindow,compListe
ner);
        mRoot->addFrameListener(FrameListener);
}
```

5. Before creating the `FrameListener`, we need to modify the compositor listener. It needs a private variable to store the number of pixels that we want our scene to have:

```
class CompositorListener1 : public Ogre::CompositorInstance::Liste
ner
{
private:
        float number;
```

6. Init this variable with 125 in the constructor:

```
public:

        CompositorListener1()
        {
                number = 125.0f;
        }
```

7. Now change the function name of the overridden function from `notifyMaterialSetup` to `notifyMaterialRender` and use the number variable instead of a fixed value to set the number of pixels:

```
void notifyMaterialRender(uint32 pass_id, MaterialPtr &mat)
{
        mat->getBestTechnique()->getPass(pass_id)-
>getFragmentProgramParameters()->setNamedConstant("numpixels",numb
er);
}
```

8. Also implement a getter and setter function for the number variable:

```
void setNumber(float num)
{
        number = num;
}

float getNumber()
{
        return number;
}
```

9. Now add `FrameListener`, which has three private variables—the input manager and the keyboard class, which we already know about, and a pointer to our compositor listener:

```cpp
class Example79FrameListener : public Ogre::FrameListener
{
private:

        OIS::InputManager* _man;
        OIS::Keyboard* _key;
        CompositorListener1* _listener;
```

10. In the constructor, we need to create our input system and save the pointer to the compositor listener:

```cpp
Example79FrameListener(RenderWindow* win,CompositorListener1*
listener)
{
        _listener = listener;

        size_t windowHnd = 0;
        std::stringstream windowHndStr;

        win->getCustomAttribute("WINDOW", &windowHnd);
        windowHndStr << windowHnd;

        OIS::ParamList pl;
        pl.insert(std::make_pair(std::string("WINDOW"),
windowHndStr.str())));

        _man = OIS::InputManager::createInputSystem( pl );
        _key = static_cast<OIS::Keyboard*>(_man->createInputObject(
OIS::OISKeyboard, false ));

}
```

11. And, as before, we need to destroy the input system we created:

```cpp
~Example79FrameListener()
{
        _man->destroyInputObject(_key);
        OIS::InputManager::destroyInputSystem(_man);
}
```

12. Override the `frameStarted()` method, and in this function, capture the keyboard input and close the application if the user pressed *Escape*:

```cpp
bool frameStarted(const Ogre::FrameEvent  &evt)
{
        _key->capture();

        if(_key->isKeyDown(OIS::KC_ESCAPE))
        {
                return false;
        }
```

13. If the user pressed the up arrow key, get the number of pixels we use right now and increase it by one. Then set and print this new value:

```cpp
if(_key->isKeyDown(OIS::KC_UP))
{
        float num = _listener->getNumber();
        num++;
        _listener->setNumber(num);

        std::cout << num << std::endl;
}
```

14. Perform the corresponding steps if the down key was pressed:

```cpp
if(_key->isKeyDown(OIS::KC_DOWN))
{
        float num = _listener->getNumber();
        num--;
        _listener->setNumber(num);

        std::cout << num << std::endl;
}
```

15. That's all. Now close the frame started function:

```cpp
        return true;
}
```

16. Compile and run the application. Also try out the effect with different numbers of pixels.

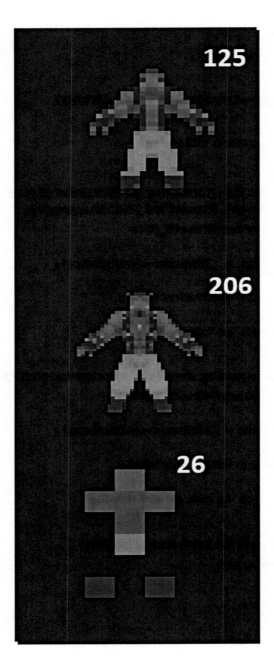

What just happened?

We extended our application to be able to control the number of pixels used for the scene with the arrow keys. Step 1 and step 4 added and created the frame listener. Step 2 inited the `FrameListener` and `CompositorListener` with `NULL` and step 3 is responsible for their destruction. Steps 5 and 6 inserted a new variable into the compositor listener, which stores the number of pixels we want our scene to have.

In step 4, we changed the method we overrode from `notifyMaterialSetup` to `notifyMaterialRender`. This was necessary because `notifyMaterialSetup` gets called only after the material has been created, but `notifyMaterialRender` gets called each time the material is going to be rendered. Because we want to be able to change the number of pixels during runtime, we need to adjust the number of pixels before each draw call. Of course, a better solution would be to only modify the parameter when the number of pixels changes. This would save some CPU time, but not that much that we need to care about it in this example.

Step 8 implemented the getter and setter methods for the number of pixels, and step 9 began implementing the frame listener. We needed the compositor listener to be able to change the number of pixels and therefore we added a private pointer variable to store it to the frame listeners.

Step 10 got the `CompositorListener` pointer and stored in the variable and initialized the input system, as we already have covered in a previous chapter. Step 11 didn't do anything new. Steps 13 and 14 used the getter and setter to manipulate the number of pixels in the compositor visitor. At the end, step 15 finished the frame listener and that was all we needed to do.

Have a go hero – reducing parameter changes

Change the application so that only when the number of pixels is changed, the parameter in the material is set to a new value. Also, don't use `notifyMaterialRender`; instead, use `notifyMaterialSetup`.

Adding a split screen

Up until now, we have seen how to add a compositor to a viewport, but there are several other interesting things that can be done with a viewport, like creating a split screen.

Time for action – adding a split screen

After playing a bit with our pixels we are now going to add a split screen

1. We don't need the whole code from the previous example. So delete the compositor listener and the frame listener.

2. We need a second camera, so create a pointer to hold it:

```
private:
        Ogre::Camera* mCamera2;
```

3. The `createScene()` function just needs to create an instance of `Sinbad.mesh` and attach it to a scene node:

```
void createScene()
{
        Ogre::SceneNode* node = mSceneMgr->getRootSceneNode()-
>createChildSceneNode();
        Ogre::Entity* ent = mSceneMgr->createEntity("Sinbad.mesh");
        node->attachObject(ent);
}
```

4. Now we need a `createCamera()` function in which we create a camera that looks at our model at (0,0,0) from (0,10,20):

```
void createCamera()
{
        mCamera = mSceneMgr->createCamera("MyCamera1");
        mCamera->setPosition(0,10,20);
        mCamera->lookAt(0,0,0);
        mCamera->setNearClipDistance(5);
```

5. Now use the new camera pointer to store another camera, which looks at the same point but now from the position (20,10,0):

```
        mCamera2 = mSceneMgr->createCamera("MyCamera2");
        mCamera2->setPosition(20,10,0);
        mCamera2->lookAt(0,0,0);
        mCamera2->setNearClipDistance(5);
}
```

6. We have the cameras, but we need the viewports, so override the
`createViewport()` method:

```
void createViewports()
{
```

7. Create a viewport that covers the left half of the render window using the
first camera:

```
Ogre::Viewport* vp = mWindow->addViewport(mCame
ra,0,0.0,0.0,0.5,1.0);
vp->setBackgroundColour(ColourValue(0.0f,0.0f,0.0f));
```

8. Then create a second viewport that covers the right half of the render window
using the second camera:

```
Ogre::Viewport* vp2 = mWindow->addViewport(mCame
ra2,1,0.5,0.0,0.5,1.0);
vp2->setBackgroundColour(ColourValue(0.0f,0.0f,0.0f));
```

9. Both cameras need the correct aspect ratio; otherwise the image
would look strange:

```
mCamera->setAspectRatio(Real(vp->getActualWidth()) / Real(vp-
>getActualHeight()));
mCamera2->setAspectRatio(Real(vp2->getActualWidth()) / Real(vp2-
>getActualHeight()));
```

10. Compile and run the application. You should see the same instance from two
different directions.

What just happened?

We created an application with two viewports; each has a camera that looks at our model instance from a different direction. Because we want to view our model from different directions, each viewport needs its own camera. Therefore, we created a new pointer in step 2 to hold our second camera. Step 3 just created a simple scene containing one model to look at. Step 4 overrode the `createCamera()` function and created our first camera, which was created at position (0,10,20) and looks at (0,0,0). This means this camera looks along the z-axis, for example, at the front of the model. Step 5 created a camera at (20,10,0), which looks along the x-axis. Step 6 overrode the `createViewports()` function, which was filled by later steps. Step 7 created the first viewport and added the first camera to the `RenderWindow`. This was done using the `addViewport()` function. As the first parameter, this function takes the camera that will deliver the image to be displayed. The second number defines which viewport has higher priority, should two viewports overlap. The viewport with the highest number is rendered if two viewports overlap. The third and fourth parameters define the beginning point of the viewport and the fifth and sixth parameters define the height and width. Each is in the range 0 to 1. The following is an image showing how our render window and viewports are set up.

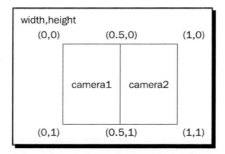

Step 9 just set the aspect ratios of each camera using the view port to get the width and height information.

Also, if we tried moving the camera with the mouse and keyboard, we might have noticed that we can only control the camera on the left viewport. This is because only the camera pointer `mCamera` is controlled from the default frame listener. If we wanted to control all cameras, we would need to modify `ExampleFrameListener`.

Have a go hero – doing more with viewports

Create an application that has four viewports—one for the front, one for the rear, one for the left, and one for the right. The result should look like the following image:

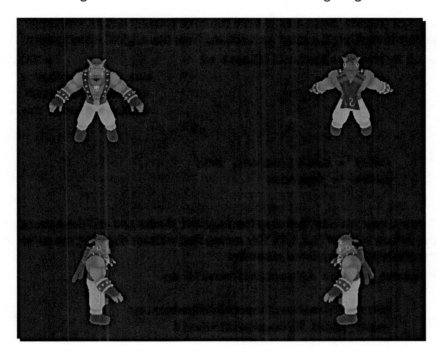

Putting it all together

We have seen how to create and apply compositors and how to create split screens using different viewports. Now we are going to combine both. In order to use the four viewports, we have to apply a compositor that multiplies the outgoing color with a `float4` as factors, and with this as the parameter, we will create a scene where we see each color channel on its own, and then the final picture, which combines them all.

Time for action – selecting a color channel

We are going to use the previous code, but we have to add and delete a lot:

1. Start with the fragment program. Besides the normal parameter, add a `float4` uniform parameter to store the color channel factors. Use these factors to multiply the color we retrieved from the original scene texture:

```
void MyFragmentShader10(float2 uv                          : TEXCOORD0,
                                 out float4 color : COLOR,
                                 uniform sampler2D texture,
                                 uniform float4 factors

                               )
{
        color = tex2D(texture, uv);
        color *= factors;
}
```

2. Create a new material that uses the fragment shader and add the parameter with the default value of (1,1,1,0). This means that without changing the parameter, the scene will be rendered normally:

```
fragment_program MyFragmentShader10 cg
{
        source Ogre3DBeginnerGuideShaders.cg
        entry_point MyFragmentShader10
        profiles ps_1_1  arbfp1

        default_params
        {
                param_named factors float4 1 1 1 0
        }


}
material Ogre3DBeginnersGuide/Comp7
{
        technique
    {
      pass
      {
                        fragment_program_ref MyFragmentShader10
              {
```

```
                }

                    texture_unit
                {
                }
            }
        }
    }
```

3. Then add a compositor that uses this material:

```
compositor Compositor9
{
    technique
    {
        texture scene target_width target_height PF_R8G8B8
        target scene
        {
            input previous
        }
        target_output
        {
            input none
            pass render_quad
            {
                material Ogre3DBeginnersGuide/Comp7
                input 0 scene
            }
        }
    }
}
```

4. We have three color channels, so we will need three compositor listeners to change the parameters accordingly. First, add the one for the red color channel. Only set the color factors in the setup of the material and we don't need them to change during runtime:

```
class CompositorListener2 : public Ogre::CompositorInstance::Liste
ner
{
public:

        void notifyMaterialSetup (uint32 pass_id, MaterialPtr &mat)
```

```
        {
                mat->getBestTechnique()->getPass(pass_id)-
>getFragmentProgramParameters()->setNamedConstant("factors",Ogre::
Vector3(1,0,0));
        }
}
```

5. Now, add the compositor for the green and blue color channels:

```
class CompositorListener3 : public Ogre::CompositorInstance::Liste
ner
{
public:

        void notifyMaterialSetup (uint32 pass_id, MaterialPtr &mat)
        {
                mat->getBestTechnique()->getPass(pass_id)-
>getFragmentProgramParameters()->setNamedConstant("factors",Ogre::
Vector3(0,1,0));
        }
};

class CompositorListener4 : public Ogre::CompositorInstance::Liste
ner
{
public:

        void notifyMaterialSetup (uint32 pass_id, MaterialPtr &mat)
        {
                mat->getBestTechnique()->getPass(pass_id)-
>getFragmentProgramParameters()->setNamedConstant("factors",Ogre::
Vector3(0,0,1));
        }
};
```

6. Instead of the camera pointer, add four viewport pointers to the application:

```
class Example83 : public ExampleApplication
{
private:

        Ogre::Viewport* vp;
        Ogre::Viewport* vp2;
        Ogre::Viewport* vp3;
        Ogre::Viewport* vp4;
```

7. Create the camera we are going to use and position it so that it looks at the front of Sinbad:

```
void createCamera()
{
        mCamera = mSceneMgr->createCamera("MyCamera1");
        mCamera->setPosition(0,10,20);
        mCamera->lookAt(0,0,0);
        mCamera->setNearClipDistance(5);

}
```

8. Adjust the `createViewport()` function to only use one camera and add the needed code for the two new viewports:

```
void createViewports()
{
        vp = mWindow->addViewport(mCamera,0,0.0,0.0,0.5,0.5);
        vp->setBackgroundColour(ColourValue(0.0f,0.0f,0.0f));

        vp2 = mWindow->addViewport(mCamera,1,0.5,0.0,0.5,0.5);
        vp2->setBackgroundColour(ColourValue(0.0f,0.0f,0.0f));

        vp3 = mWindow->addViewport(mCamera,2,0.0,0.5,0.5,0.5);
        vp3->setBackgroundColour(ColourValue(0.0f,0.0f,0.0f));

        vp4 = mWindow->addViewport(mCamera,3,0.5,0.5,0.5,0.5);
        vp4->setBackgroundColour(ColourValue(0.0f,0.0f,0.0f));

        mCamera->setAspectRatio(Real(vp->getActualWidth()) /
Real(vp->getActualHeight()));
}
```

9. Add three pointers for storing the Compositor Listeners we have created above the application:

```
CompositorListener2* compListener;
CompositorListener3* compListener2;
CompositorListener4* compListener3;
```

10. Init each of them with NULL in the constructor:

```
Example83()
{
        compListener = NULL;
        compListener2 = NULL;
        compListener3 = NULL;

}
```

11. And, of course, delete them in the destructor:

```
~Example83()
{
            if(compListener)
        {
            delete compListener;
        }
        if(compListener2)
        {
            delete compListener2;
        }
        if(compListener3)
        {
            delete compListener3;
        }
}
```

12. In the `createScene()` function, after the creation of the model instance and the scene node, add the code needed to add the compositor to our first viewport , enable it, and attach to it the compositor listener that only allows the red color channel to be rendered:

```
Ogre::CompositorManager::getSingleton().addCompositor(vp,
"Compositor9");

Ogre::CompositorManager::getSingleton().setCompositorEnabled(vp,
"Compositor9", true);

Ogre::CompositorInstance* comp =  Ogre::CompositorManager::getSing
leton().getCompositorChain(vp)->getCompositor("Compositor9");
compListener = new CompositorListener2();
comp->addListener(compListener);
```

13. Do the same for the second and third viewports using the green and blue only compositor listeners:

```
Ogre::CompositorManager::getSingleton().addCompositor(vp2,
"Compositor9");

Ogre::CompositorManager::getSingleton().setCompositorEnabled(vp2,
"Compositor9", true);

Ogre::CompositorInstance* comp2 =  Ogre::CompositorManager::getSin
gleton().getCompositorChain(vp2)->getCompositor("Compositor9");
compListener2 = new CompositorListener3();
comp2->addListener(compListener2);
```

```
Ogre::CompositorManager::getSingleton().addCompositor(vp3,
"Compositor9");
Ogre::CompositorManager::getSingleton().setCompositorEnabled(vp3,
"Compositor9", true);

Ogre::CompositorInstance* comp3 = Ogre::CompositorManager::getSin
gleton().getCompositorChain(vp3)->getCompositor("Compositor9");
compListener3 = new CompositorListener4();
comp3->addListener(compListener3);
```

14. Now run and compile the application. You should see the four identical images, only with different color channels rendered. At the top left, there is only the red color channel visible; on the top right, only the green; on the bottom left, the blue; and on the bottom right, the image with all the color channels:

What just happened?

We used the knowledge we gathered from the examples in this chapter to create an application that uses four viewports and one compositor in combination with three compositor listeners to see each color channel on its own and the combined result. Nothing really new has happened in this example; if needed, consult the other examples to understand this one.

Summary

We learned a lot in this chapter about compositors and viewports.

Specifically, we covered:

- How to create compositor scripts and how to add them to our scene
- How to manipulate our scene using compositors and fragment shaders
- The parameters for shaders and how to change their values in material scripts or directly in the application code
- How to combine compositors to save us the work of rewriting the same code over and over again
- Combining topics we have learned previously to create a compositor that is controlled by user input

We now have covered a lot of Ogre 3D; only one really important topic is left. Up until now, we have relied on ExampleApplication. In the next chapter, we are going to write our own ExampleApplication.

9

The Ogre 3D Startup Sequence

We have covered a lot of ground in the progress of this book. This chapter is going to cover one of the few topics left: how to create our own application without relying on the ExampleApplication. *After we have covered this topic, this chapter is going to repeat some of the topics from the previous chapters to make a demo of the things we have learned using our new open application class.*

In this chapter, we will:

- ◆ Learn how to start Ogre 3D ourselves
- ◆ Parse resources.cfg to load the models we need
- ◆ Combine things from the previous chapters to make a small demo application showing off the things we have learned

So let's get on with it...

Starting Ogre 3D

Up until now, the ExampleApplication class has started and initialized Ogre 3D for us; now we are going to do it ourselves.

Time for action – starting Ogre 3D

This time we are working on a blank sheet.

1. Start with an empty code file, include `Ogre3d.h`, and create an empty main function:

```
#include "Ogre\Ogre.h"

int main (void)
{
  return 0;
}
```

2. Create an instance of the Ogre 3D `Root` class; this class needs the name of the `"plugin.cfg"`:

```
Ogre::Root* root = new Ogre::Root("plugins_d.cfg");
```

3. If the config dialog can't be shown or the user cancels it, close the application:

```
if(!root->showConfigDialog())
{
  return -1;
}
```

4. Create a render window:

```
Ogre::RenderWindow* window = root->initialise(true,"Ogre3D
Beginners Guide");
```

5. Next create a new scene manager:

```
Ogre::SceneManager* sceneManager = root-
>createSceneManager(Ogre::ST_GENERIC);
```

6. Create a camera and name it `camera`:

```
Ogre::Camera* camera = sceneManager->createCamera("Camera");
camera->setPosition(Ogre::Vector3(0,0,50));
camera->lookAt(Ogre::Vector3(0,0,0));
camera->setNearClipDistance(5);
```

7. With this camera, create a `viewport` and set the background color to black:

```
Ogre::Viewport* viewport = window->addViewport(camera);
viewport->setBackgroundColour(Ogre::ColourValue(0.0,0.0,0.0));
```

8. Now, use this viewport to set the aspect ratio of the camera:

```
camera->setAspectRatio(Ogre::Real(viewport->getActualWidth())/
Ogre::Real(viewport->getActualHeight()));
```

9. Finally, tell the root to start rendering:

```
root->startRendering();
```

10. Compile and run the application; you should see the normal config dialog and then a black window. This window can't be closed by pressing *Escape* because we haven't added key handling yet. You can close the application by pressing *CTRL+C* in the console the application has been started from.

What just happened?

We created our first Ogre 3D application without the help of the `ExampleApplication`. Because we aren't using the `ExampleApplication` any longer, we had to include `Ogre3D.h`, which was previously included by `ExampleApplication.h`. Before we can do anything with Ogre 3D, we need a `root` instance. The `root` class is a class that manages the higher levels of Ogre 3D, creates and saves the factories used for creating other objects, loads and unloads the needed plugins, and a lot more. We gave the `root` instance one parameter: the name of the file that defines which plugins to load. The following is the complete signature of the constructor:

```
Root(const String & pluginFileName = "plugins.cfg",const String &
configFileName = "ogre.cfg",const String & logFileName = "Ogre.log")
```

Besides the name for the plugin configuration file, the function also needs the name of the Ogre configuration and the log file. We needed to change the first file name because we are using the debug version of our application and therefore want to load the debug plugins. The default value is `plugins.cfg`, which is true for the release folder of the Ogre 3D SDK, but our application is running in the debug folder where the filename is `plugins_d.cfg`.

`ogre.cfg` contains the settings for starting the Ogre application that we selected in the config dialog. This saves the user from making the same changes every time he/she starts our application. With this file Ogre 3D can remember his choices and use them as defaults for the next start. This file is created if it didn't exist, so we don't append an _d to the filename and can use the default; the same is true for the log file.

Using the `root` instance, we let Ogre 3D show the config dialog to the user in step 3. When the user cancels the dialog or anything goes wrong, we return -1 and with this the application closes. Otherwise, we created a new render window and a new scene manager in step 4. Using the scene manager, we created a camera, and with the camera we created the viewport; then, using the viewport, we calculated the aspect ratio for the camera. The creation of camera and viewport shouldn't be anything new; we have already done that in Chapter 3, *Camera, Light, and Shadow*. After creating all requirements, we told the `root` instance to start rendering, so our result would be visible. Following is a diagram showing which object was needed to create the other:

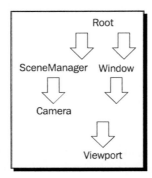

Adding resources

We have now created our first Ogre 3D application, which doesn't need the `ExampleApplication`. But one important thing is missing: we haven't loaded and rendered a model yet.

Time for action – loading the Sinbad mesh

We have our application, now let's add a model.

1. After setting the aspect ratio and before starting the rendering, add the `zip` archive containing the Sinbad model to our resources:

   ```
   Ogre::ResourceGroupManager::getSingleton().
   addResourceLocation("../../Media/packs/Sinbad.zip","Zip");
   ```

2. We don't want to index more resources at the moment, so index all added resources now:

   ```
   Ogre::ResourceGroupManager::getSingleton().
   initialiseAllResourceGroups();
   ```

3. Now create an instance of the Sinbad mesh and add it to the scene:

```
Ogre::Entity* ent = sceneManager->createEntity("Sinbad.mesh");
sceneManager->getRootSceneNode()->attachObject(ent);
```

4. Compile and run the application; you should see Sinbad in the middle of the screen:

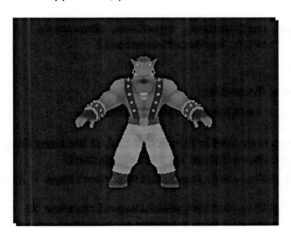

What just happened?

We used the `ResourceGroupManager` to index the `zip` archive containing the Sinbad mesh and texture files, and after this was done, we told it to load the data with the `createEntity()` call in step 3.

Using resources.cfg

Adding a new line of code for each `zip` archive or folder we want to load is a tedious task and we should try to avoid it. The `ExampleApplication` used a configuration file called `resources.cfg` in which each folder or `zip` archive was listed, and all the content was loaded using this file. Let's replicate this behavior.

Time for action – using resources.cfg to load our models

Using our previous application, we are now going to parse the `resources.cfg`.

1. Replace the loading of the `zip` archive with an instance of a config file pointing at the `resources_d.cfg`:

```
Ogre::ConfigFile cf;
cf.load(«resources_d.cfg»);
```

2. First get the iterator, which goes over each section of the config file:

```
Ogre::ConfigFile::SectionIterator sectionIter =
cf.getSectionIterator();
```

3. Define three strings to save the data we are going to extract from the config file and iterate over each section:

```
Ogre::String sectionName, typeName, dataname;
while (sectionIter.hasMoreElements())
{
```

4. Get the name of the section:

```
sectionName = sectionIter.peekNextKey();
```

5. Get the settings contained in the section and, at the same time, advance the section iterator; also create an iterator for the settings itself:

```
Ogre::ConfigFile::SettingsMultiMap *settings = sectionIter.
getNext();
Ogre::ConfigFile::SettingsMultiMap::iterator i;
```

6. Iterate over each setting in the section:

```
for (i = settings->begin(); i != settings->end(); ++i)
{
```

7. Use the iterator to get the name and the type of the resources:

```
typeName = i->first;
dataname = i->second;
```

8. Use the resource name, type, and section name to add it to the resource index:

```
Ogre::ResourceGroupManager::getSingleton().
addResourceLocation(dataname, typeName, sectionName);
```

9. Compile and run the application, and you should see the same scene as before.

What just happened?

In the first step, we used another helper class of Ogre 3D, called `ConfigFile`. This class is used to easily load and parse simple configuration files, which consist of name-value pairs. By using an instance of the `ConfigFile` class, we loaded the `resources_d.cfg`. We hardcoded the filename with the debug postfix; this isn't good practice and in a production application we would use `#ifdef` to change the filename depending on the debug or release mode. `ExampleApplication` does this; let's take a look at `ExampleApplication.h` line 384:

```
#if OGRE_DEBUG_MODE
        cf.load(mResourcePath + "resources_d.cfg");
#else
    cf.load(mResourcePath + "resources.cfg");
#endif
```

Structure of a configuration file

The configuration file loaded by the helper class follows a simple structure; here is an example from `resource.cfg`. Of course your `resource.cfg` will consist of different paths:

```
[General]
FileSystem=D:/programming/ogre/ogre_trunk_1_7/Samples/Media
```

`[General]` starts a section, which goes on until another `[sectionname]` occurs in the file. Each configuration file can contain a lot of sections; in step 2 we created an iterator to iterate over all the sections in the file and in step 3 we used a while loop, which runs until we have processed each section.

A section consists of several settings and each setting assigns a key a value. We assign the key `FileSystem` the value `D:/programming/ogre/ogre_trunk_1_7/Samples/Media`. In step 4, we created an iterator so we can iterate over each setting. The settings are internally called name-value pairs. We iterate over this map and for each entry we use the map key as the type of the resource and the data we use as the path. Using the section name as resource group, we added the resource using the resource group manager in step 8. Once we had parsed the complete file, we indexed all the files.

Creating an application class

We now have the basis for our own Ogre 3D application, but all the code is in the main function, which isn't really desirable for reusing the code.

Time for action – creating a class

Using the previously applied code we are now going to create a class to separate the Ogre code from the main function.

1. Create the class `MyApplication`, which has two private pointers, one to a Ogre 3D `SceneManager` and the other to the `Root` class:

```
class MyApplication
{
private:
  Ogre::SceneManager* _sceneManager;
Ogre::Root* _root;
```

2. The rest of this class should be public:

```
public:
```

3. Create a `loadResources()` function, which loads the `resources.cfg` configuration file:

```
void loadResources()
{
  Ogre::ConfigFile cf;
  cf.load(«resources_d.cfg»);
```

4. Iterate over the sections of the configuration file:

```
Ogre::ConfigFile::SectionIterator sectionIter =
cf.getSectionIterator();
Ogre::String sectionName, typeName, dataname;
while (sectionIter.hasMoreElements())
{
```

5. Get the section name and the iterator for the settings:

```
sectionName = sectionIter.peekNextKey();
Ogre::ConfigFile::SettingsMultiMap *settings = sectionIter.
getNext();
Ogre::ConfigFile::SettingsMultiMap::iterator i;
```

6. Iterate over the settings and add each resource:

```
    for (i = settings->begin(); i != settings->end(); ++i)
    {
      typeName = i->first;
      dataname = i->second;
      Ogre::ResourceGroupManager::getSingleton().
addResourceLocation(
      dataname, typeName, sectionName);
```

```
    }
  }

  Ogre::ResourceGroupManager::getSingleton().
  initialiseAllResourceGroups();
}
```

7. Also create a `startup()` function, which creates an Ogre 3D `root` class instance using the `plugins.cfg`:

```
int startup()
{
  _root = new Ogre::Root(«plugins_d.cfg»);
```

8. Show the config dialog and when the user quits it, return `-1` to close the application:

```
if(!_root->showConfigDialog())
{
  return -1;
}
```

9. Create the `RenderWindow` and the `SceneManager`:

```
Ogre::RenderWindow* window = _root->initialise(true,"Ogre3D
Beginners Guide");
_sceneManager = root->createSceneManager(Ogre::ST_GENERIC);
```

10. Create a `camera` and a `viewport`:

```
Ogre::Camera* camera = _sceneManager->createCamera("Camera");
camera->setPosition(Ogre::Vector3(0,0,50));
camera->lookAt(Ogre::Vector3(0,0,0));
camera->setNearClipDistance(5);

Ogre::Viewport* viewport = window->addViewport(camera);
viewport->setBackgroundColour(Ogre::ColourValue(0.0,0.0,0.0));
camera->setAspectRatio(Ogre::Real(viewport->getActualWidth())/
Ogre::Real(viewport->getActualHeight()));
```

11. Call the function to load our resources and then a function to create a scene; after that, Ogre 3D starts rendering:

```
loadResources();
createScene();
_root->startRendering();
return 0;
```

12. Then create the `createScene()` function, which contains the code for creating the `SceneNode` **and the** `Entity`:

```
void createScene()
{
  Ogre::Entity* ent = _sceneManager->createEntity(«Sinbad.mesh»);
  _sceneManager->getRootSceneNode()->attachObject(ent);
}
```

13. We need the constructor to set both the pointers to NULL so we can delete it even if it hasn't been assigned a value:

```
MyApplication()
{
  _sceneManager = NULL;
_root = NULL;
}
```

14. We need to delete the `root` instance when our application instance is destroyed, so implement a destructor which does this:

```
~MyApplication()
{
  delete _root;
}
```

15. The only thing left to do is to adjust the main function:

```
int main (void)
{
  MyApplication app;
  app.startup();
  return 0;
}
```

16. Compile and run the application; the scene should be unchanged.

What just happened?

We refactored our starting codebase so that different functionalities are better organized. We also added a destructor so our created instances would be deleted when our application is closed. One problem is that our destructor won't be called; because `startup()` never returns, there is no way to close our application. We need to add a `FrameListener` to tell Ogre 3D to stop rendering.

Adding a FrameListener

We have already used the `ExampleFrameListener`; this time we are going to use our own implementation of the interface.

Time for action – adding a FrameListener

Using the code from before we are going to add our own `FrameListener` implementation

1. Create a new class called `MyFrameListener` exposing three publicly visible event handler functions:

```
class MyFrameListener : public Ogre::FrameListener
{
public:
```

2. First, implement the `frameStarted` function, which for now returns `false` to close the application:

```
bool frameStarted(const Ogre::FrameEvent& evt)
{
  return false;
}
```

3. We also need a `frameEnded` function, which also returns `false`:

```
bool frameEnded(const Ogre::FrameEvent& evt)
{
  return false;
}
```

4. The last function we implement is the `frameRenderingQueued` function, which also returns `false`:

```
bool frameRenderingQueued(const Ogre::FrameEvent& evt)
{
  return false;
}
```

5. The main class needs a point to store the `FrameListener`:

```
MyFrameListener* _listener;
```

6. Remember that the constructor needs to set the initial value of the listener to `NULL`:

```
_listener = NULL;
```

7. Let the destructor delete the instance:

```
delete _listener;
```

8. At last, create a new instance of the `FrameListener` and add it to the root object; this should happen in the `startup()` function:

```
_listener = new MyFrameListener();
_root->addFrameListener(_listener);
```

9. Compile and run the application; it should be closed directly.

What just happened?

We created our own `FrameListener` class, which didn't rely on the `ExampleFrameListener` implementation. This time we inherited directly from the `FrameListener` interface. This interface consists of three virtual functions, which we implemented. We already knew the `frameStarted` function, but the other two are new. All three functions return `false`, which is an indicator to Ogre 3D to stop rendering and close the application. Using our implementation, we added a `FrameListener` to the `root` instance and started the application; not surprisingly, it closed directly.

Investigating the FrameListener functionality

Our `FrameListener` implementation has three functions; each is called at a different point in time. We are going to investigate in which sequence they are called.

Time for action – experimenting with the FrameListener implementation

Using the console printing we are going to inspect when the `FrameListener` is called.

1. First let each function print a message to the console when it is called:

```
bool frameStarted(const Ogre::FrameEvent& evt)
{
  std::cout << «Frame started» << std::endl;
  return false;
}
bool frameEnded(const Ogre::FrameEvent& evt)
{
  std::cout << «Frame ended» << std::endl;
  return false;
}
bool frameRenderingQueued(const Ogre::FrameEvent& evt)
```

```
{
  std::cout << «Frame queued» << std::endl;
  return false;
}
```

2. Compile and run the application; in the console you should find the first string—
Frame started.

What just happened?

We added a "debug" output to each of the `FrameListener` functions to see which function
is getting called. Running the application, we noticed that only the first debug message is
printed. The reason is that the `frameStarted` function returns `false`, which is a signal for
the `root` instance to close the application.

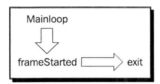

Now that we know what happens when `frameStarted()` returns `false`, let's see what
happens when `frameStarted()` returns `true`.

Time for action – returning true in the frameStarted function

Now we are going to modify the behavior of our `FrameListener` to see how this changed
its behavior.

1. Change `frameStarted` to return `true`:

```
bool frameStarted(const Ogre::FrameEvent& evt)
{
  std::cout << «Frame started» << std::endl;
  return true;
}
```

2. Compile and run the application. Before the application closes directly, you will see
a short glimpse of the rendered scene and there should be the two following lines in
the output:

Frame started

Frame queued

What just happened?

Now, the `frameStarted` function returns `true` and this lets Ogre 3D continue to render until `false` is returned by the `frameRenderingQueued` function. We see a scene this time because directly after the `frameRenderingQueued` function is called, the render buffers are swapped before the application gets the possibility to close itself.

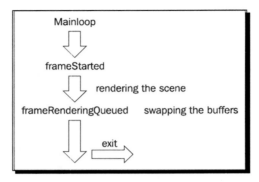

Double buffering

When a scene is rendered, it isn't normally rendered directly to the buffer, which is displayed on the monitor. Normally, the scene is rendered to a second buffer and when the rendering is finished, the buffers are swapped. This is done to prevent some artifacts, which can be created if we render to the same buffer, which is displayed on the monitor. The `FrameListener` function, `frameRenderingQueued`, is called after the scene has been rendered to the back buffer, the buffer which isn't displayed at the moment. Before the buffers are swapped, the rendering result is already created but not yet displayed. Directly after the `frameRenderingQueued` function is called, the buffers get swapped and then the application gets the return value and closes itself. That's the reason why we see an image this time.

Now, we will see what happens when `frameRenderingQueued` also returns `true`.

Time for action – returning true in the frameRenderingQueued function

Once again we modify the code to test the behavior of the Frame Listener.

1. Change `frameRenderingQueued` to return `true`:

```
bool frameRenderingQueued (const Ogre::FrameEvent& evt)
{
  std::cout << «Frame queued» << std::endl;
  return true;
}
```

2. Compile and run the application. You should see Sinbad for a short period of time before the application closes, and the following three lines should be in the console output:

Frame started

Frame queued

Frame ended

What just happened?

Now that the `frameRenderingQueued` handler returns `true`, it will let Ogre 3D continue to render until the `frameEnded` handler returns `false`.

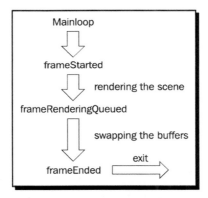

Like in the last example, the render buffers were swapped, so we saw the scene for a short period of time. After the frame was rendered, the `frameEnded` function returned `false`, which closes the application and, in this case, doesn't change anything from our perspective.

Time for action – returning true in the frameEnded function

Now let's test the last of three possibilities.

1. Change `frameRenderingQueued` to return `true`:

```
bool frameEnded (const Ogre::FrameEvent& evt)
{
  std::cout << «Frame ended» << std::endl;
  return true;
}
```

2. Compile and run the application. You should see the scene with Sinbad and an endless repetition of the following three lines:

Frame started

Frame queued

Frame ended

What just happened?

Now, all event handlers returned `true` and, therefore, the application will never be closed; it would run forever as long as we aren't going to close the application ourselves.

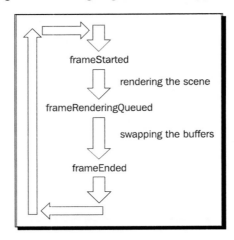

Adding input

We have an application running forever and have to force it to close; that's not neat. Let's add input and the possibility to close the application by pressing *Escape.*

Time for action – adding input

Now that we know how the `FrameListener` works, let's add some input.

1. We need to include the `OIS` header file to use `OIS`:

```
#include "OIS\OIS.h"
```

2. Remove all functions from the `FrameListener` and add two private members to store the `InputManager` and the `Keyboard`:

```
OIS::InputManager* _InputManager;
```

```
OIS::Keyboard* _Keyboard;
```

3. The `FrameListener` needs a pointer to the `RenderWindow` to initialize `OIS`, so we need a constructor, which takes the window as a parameter:

```
MyFrameListener(Ogre::RenderWindow* win)
{
```

4. `OIS` will be initialized using a list of parameters, we also need a window handle in string form for the parameter list; create the three needed variables to store the data:

```
OIS::ParamList parameters;
unsigned int windowHandle = 0;
std::ostringstream windowHandleString;
```

5. Get the handle of the `RenderWindow` and convert it into a string:

```
win->getCustomAttribute("WINDOW", &windowHandle);
windowHandleString << windowHandle;
```

6. Add the string containing the window handle to the parameter list using the key `"WINDOW"`:

```
parameters.insert(std::make_pair("WINDOW", windowHandleString.
str()));
```

7. Use the parameter list to create the `InputManager`:

```
_InputManager = OIS::InputManager::createInputSystem(parameters);
```

8. With the manager create the keyboard:

```
_Keyboard = static_cast<OIS::Keyboard*>(_InputManager-
>createInputObject( OIS::OISKeyboard, false ));
```

9. What we created in the constructor, we need to destroy in the destructor:

```
~MyFrameListener()
{
  _InputManager->destroyInputObject(_Keyboard);
  OIS::InputManager::destroyInputSystem(_InputManager);
}
```

10. Create a new `frameStarted` function, which captures the current state of the keyboard, and if *Escape* is pressed, it returns `false`; otherwise, it returns `true`:

```
bool frameStarted(const Ogre::FrameEvent& evt)
{
  _Keyboard->capture();
  if(_Keyboard->isKeyDown(OIS::KC_ESCAPE))
```

```
  {
    return false;
  }
  return true;
}
```

11. The last thing to do is to change the instantiation of the `FrameListener` to use a pointer to the render window in the `startup` function:

```
_listener = new MyFrameListener(window);
_root->addFrameListener(_listener);
```

12. Compile and run the application. You should see the scene and now be able to close it by pressing the *Escape* key.

What just happened?

We added input processing capabilities to our `FrameListener` the same way we did in *Chapter 4*, *Getting User Input and using the Frame Listener*. The only difference is that this time, we didn't use any example classes, but our own versions.

Pop quiz – the three event handlers

Which three functions offer the `FrameListener` interface and at which point is each of these functions called?

Our own main loop

We have used the `startRendering` function to fire up our application. After this, the only way we knew when a frame was rendered was by relying on the `FrameListener`. But sometimes it is not possible or desirable to give up the control over the main loop; for such cases, Ogre 3D provides another method, which doesn't require us to give up the control over the main loop.

Time for action – using our own rendering loop

Using the code from before we are now going to use our own rendering loop.

1. Our application needs to know if it should keep running or not; add a `Boolean` as a private member of the application to remember the state:

```
bool _keepRunning;
```

2. Remove the `startRendering` function call in the `startup` function.

3. Add a new function called `renderOneFrame`, which calls the `renderOneFrame` function of the `root` instance and saves the return value in the `_keepRunning` member variable. Before this call, add a function to process all window events:

```
void renderOneFrame()
{
  Ogre::WindowEventUtilities::messagePump();
  _keepRunning = _root->renderOneFrame();
}
```

4. Add a getter for the `_keepRunning` member variable:

```
bool keepRunning()
{
  return _keepRunning;
}
```

5. Add a `while` loop to the main function, which keeps running as long as the `keepRunning` function returns `true`. In the body of the loop, call the `renderOneFrame` function of the application.

```
while(app.keepRunning())
{
  app.renderOneFrame();
}
```

6. Compile and run the application. There shouldn't be any noticeable difference to the last example.

What just happened?

We moved the control of the main loop from Ogre 3D to our application. Before this change, Ogre 3D used an internal main loop over which we hadn't any control and had to rely on the `FrameListener` to get notified if a frame was rendered.

Now we have our own main loop. To get there, we needed a `Boolean` member variable, which signals if the application wishes to keep running or not; this variable was added in step 1. Step 2 removed the `startRendering` function call so we wouldn't hand over the control to Ogre 3D. In step 3, we created a function, which first calls a helper function of Ogre 3D, which processes all window events we might have gotten from the operating system. It then sends all messages we might have created since the last frame, and therefore makes the application "well-behaved" in the context of the host windowing system.

After this we call the Ogre 3D function `renderOneFrame`, which does exactly what the name suggests: it renders the frame and also calls the `frameStarted`, `frameRenderingQueued`, and `frameEnded` event handler of each registered `FrameListener` and returns `false` if any of these functions returned `false`. Since we assign the return value of the function to the `_keepRunning` member variable, we can use this variable to check if the application should keep running. When `renderOneFrame` returns a `false`, we know some `FrameListener` wants to close the application and we set the `_keepRunning` variable to `false`. The fourth step just added a getter for the `_keepRunning` member variable.

In step 5, we used the `_keepRunning` variable as the condition for the `while` loop. This means the `while` loop will run as long as `_keepRunning` is `true`, which will be the case until one `FrameListener` returns `false`, which then will result in the `while` loop to exit and with this the whole application will be closed. Inside the `while` loop we call the `renderOneFrame` function of the application to update the render window with the newest render result. This is all we needed to create our own main loop.

Adding a camera (again)

We have already implemented a camera in *Chapter 4, Getting User Input and Using the Frame Listener*, but, nevertheless, we want a controllable camera in our own implementation of the frame listener, so here we go.

Time for action – adding a frame listener

Using our `FrameListener` we are going to add a user controlled camera.

1. To control the camera we need a mouse interface, a pointer to the camera, and a variable defining the speed at which our camera should move as a member variable of our `FrameListener`:

    ```
    OIS::Mouse* _Mouse;
    Ogre::Camera* _Cam;
    float _movementspeed;
    ```

2. Adjust the constructor and add the camera pointer as the new parameter and set the movement speed to 50:

    ```
    MyFrameListener(Ogre::RenderWindow* win,Ogre::Camera* cam)
    {
      _Cam = cam;
      _movementspeed = 50.0f;
    ```

3. Init the mouse using the `InputManager`:

```
_Mouse = static_cast<OIS::Mouse*>(_InputManager-
>createInputObject( OIS::OISMouse, false ));
```

4. And remember to destroy it in the destructor:

```
_InputManager->destroyInputObject(_Mouse);
```

5. Add the code to move the camera using the *W, A, S, D* keys and the movement speed to the `frameStarted` event handler:

```
Ogre::Vector3 translate(0,0,0);
if(_Keyboard->isKeyDown(OIS::KC_W))
{
   translate += Ogre::Vector3(0,0,-1);
}
if(_Keyboard->isKeyDown(OIS::KC_S))
{
   translate += Ogre::Vector3(0,0,1);
}
if(_Keyboard->isKeyDown(OIS::KC_A))
{
   translate += Ogre::Vector3(-1,0,0);
}
if(_Keyboard->isKeyDown(OIS::KC_D))
{
   translate += Ogre::Vector3(1,0,0);
}
_Cam->moveRelative(translate*evt.timeSinceLastFrame * _
movementspeed);
```

6. Now do the same for the mouse control:

```
_Mouse->capture();
float rotX = _Mouse->getMouseState().X.rel * evt.
timeSinceLastFrame* -1;
float rotY = _Mouse->getMouseState().Y.rel * evt.
timeSinceLastFrame * -1;
_Cam->yaw(Ogre::Radian(rotX));
_Cam->pitch(Ogre::Radian(rotY));
```

7. The last thing to do is to change the instantiation of the `FrameListener`:

```
_listener = new MyFrameListener(window,camera);
```

8. Compile and run the application. The scene should be unchanged but now we can control the camera:

What just happened?

We used our knowledge from the previous chapters to add a user-controlled camera. The next step will be to add compositors and other features to make our application more interesting and to leverage some of the techniques we learned along the way.

Adding compositors

Previously, we have created three compositors, which we are now going to add to our application with the capability to turn each one off and on using keyboard input.

Time for action – adding compositors

Having almost finished our application, we are going to add compositors to make the application more interesting.

1. We are going to use compositors in our `FrameListener`, so we need a member variable containing the viewport:

   ```
   Ogre::Viewport* _viewport;
   ```

2. We also are going to need to save which compositor is turned on; add three `Booleans` for this task:

   ```
   bool _comp1, _comp2, _comp3;
   ```

3. We are going to use keyboard input to switch the compositors on and off. To be able to differentiate between key presses, we need to know the previous state of the key:

```
bool _down1, _down2, _down3;
```

4. Change the constructor of the `FrameListener` to take the viewport as a parameter:

```
MyFrameListener(Ogre::RenderWindow* win,Ogre::Camera*
cam,Ogre::Viewport* viewport)
```

5. Assign the viewport pointer to the member and assign the Boolean value their starting value:

```
_viewport = viewport;

_comp1 = false;
_comp2 = false;
_comp3 = false;

_down1 = false;
_down2 = false;
_down3 = false;
```

6. If the key number *1* is pressed and it wasn't pressed before, change the state of the key to pressed, flip the state of the compositor, and use the flipped value to enable or disable the compositor. This code goes into the `frameStarted` function:

```
if (_Keyboard->isKeyDown(OIS::KC_1) && ! _down1)
{
  _down1 = true;
  _comp1 = !comp1;
  Ogre::CompositorManager::getSingleton().setCompositorEnabled(_
viewport, "Compositor2", _comp1);
}
```

7. Do the same for the other two compositors we are going to have:

```
if (_Keyboard->isKeyDown(OIS::KC_2) && ! _down2)
{
  _down2 = true;
  _comp2 = !comp2;
  Ogre::CompositorManager::getSingleton().setCompositorEnabled(_
viewport, "Compositor3", _comp2);
}
if (_Keyboard->isKeyDown(OIS::KC_3) && ! _down3)
{
  _down3 = true;
  _comp3 = !comp3;
```

```
Ogre::CompositorManager::getSingleton().setCompositorEnabled(_
viewport, "Compositor7", _comp3);
}
```

8. If a key is no longer pressed, we need to change the state of the key:

```
if(!_Keyboard->isKeyDown(OIS::KC_1))
{
  _down1 = false;
}
if(!_Keyboard->isKeyDown(OIS::KC_2))
{
  _down2 = false;
}
if(!_Keyboard->isKeyDown(OIS::KC_3))
{
  _down3 = false;
}
```

9. In the `startup()` function, add the three compositors to the viewport to the end of the function:

```
Ogre::CompositorManager::getSingleton().addCompositor(viewport,
"Compositor2");
Ogre::CompositorManager::getSingleton().addCompositor(viewport,
"Compositor3");
Ogre::CompositorManager::getSingleton().addCompositor(viewport,
"Compositor7");
```

10. Remember to change the instantiation of the `FrameListener` to add the viewport pointer as parameter:

```
_listener = new MyFrameListener(window,camera,viewport);
```

11. Compile and run the application. Using the *1, 2, 3* keys, you should be able to turn different compositors on and off. The *1* key is for making the image black and white, the *2* key inverts the image, and the *3* key makes the image look like it has a smaller resolution; you can combine all of the effect the way you like:

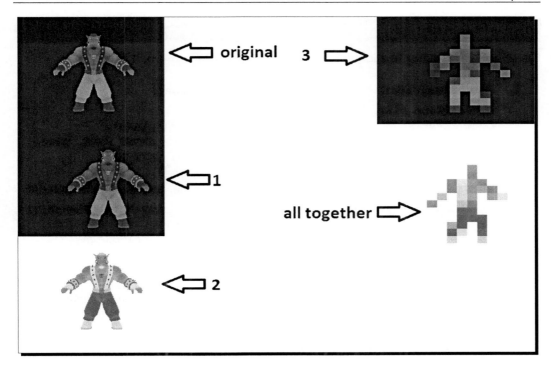

What just happened?

We added the compositors we wrote in the chapter about and made it possible to turn them on and off using the *1*, *2*, and *3* keys. To combine the compositors, we used the fact that Ogre 3D automatically chains compositors if more than one is enabled.

Adding a plane

Without a reference to where the ground is, navigation in 3D space is difficult, so once again let's add a floor plane.

Time for action – adding a plane and a light

Everything we are going to add this time is going in the `createScene()` function:

1. As we already know we need a plane definition, so add one:

```
Ogre::Plane plane(Ogre::Vector3::UNIT_Y, -5);
Ogre::MeshManager::getSingleton().createPlane("plane",
  Ogre::ResourceGroupManager::DEFAULT_RESOURCE_GROUP_NAME, plane,
  1500,1500,200,200,true,1,5,5,Ogre::Vector3::UNIT_Z);
```

2. Then create an instance of this plane, add it to the scene, and change the material:

```
Ogre::Entity* ground= _sceneManager->createEntity("LightPlaneEnti
ty", "plane");
_sceneManager->getRootSceneNode()->createChildSceneNode()-
>attachObject(ground);
ground->setMaterialName("Examples/BeachStones");
```

3. Also we would like to have some light in the scene; add one directional light:

```
Ogre::Light* light = _sceneManager->createLight("Light1");
light->setType(Ogre::Light::LT_DIRECTIONAL);
light->setDirection(Ogre::Vector3(1,-1,0));
```

4. And some shadows would be nice:

```
_sceneManager->setShadowTechnique(Ogre::SHADOWTYPE_STENCIL_
ADDITIVE);
```

5. Compile and run the application. You should see a plane with a stone texture and on top the Sinbad instance throwing a shadow on the plane.

What just happened?

Again, we used our previously gained knowledge to create a plane, light, and add shadows to the scene.

Adding user control

We have our model instance on a plane, but we can't move it yet; let's change this now.

Time for action – controlling the model with the arrow keys

Now we are going to add interactivity to the scene by adding the user control to the movements of the model.

1. The `FrameListener` needs two new members: one pointer to the node we want to move, and one float indicating the movement speed:

```
float _WalkingSpeed;
Ogre::SceneNode* _node;
```

2. The pointer to the node is passed to us in the constructor:

```
MyFrameListener(Ogre::RenderWindow* win,Ogre::Camera*
cam,Ogre::Viewport* viewport,Ogre::SceneNode* node)
```

3. Assign the node pointer to the member variable and set the walking speed to 50:

```
_WalkingSpeed = 50.0f;
_node = node;
```

4. In the `frameStarted` function we need two new variables, which will hold the rotation and the translation the user wants to apply to the node:

```
Ogre::Vector3 SinbadTranslate(0,0,0);
float _rotation = 0.0f;
```

5. Then we need code to calculate the translation and rotation depending on which arrow key the user has pressed:

```
if(_Keyboard->isKeyDown(OIS::KC_UP))
{
  SinbadTranslate += Ogre::Vector3(0,0,-1);
  _rotation = 3.14f;
}
if(_Keyboard->isKeyDown(OIS::KC_DOWN))
{
  SinbadTranslate += Ogre::Vector3(0,0,1);
  _rotation = 0.0f;
}
if(_Keyboard->isKeyDown(OIS::KC_LEFT))
{
  SinbadTranslate += Ogre::Vector3(-1,0,0);
  _rotation = -1.57f;
}
if(_Keyboard->isKeyDown(OIS::KC_RIGHT))
{
  SinbadTranslate += Ogre::Vector3(1,0,0);
  _rotation = 1.57f;
}
```

6. Then we need to apply the translation and rotation to the node:

```
_node->translate(SinbadTranslate * evt.timeSinceLastFrame * _
WalkingSpeed);
_node->resetOrientation();
_node->yaw(Ogre::Radian(_rotation));
```

7. The application itself also needs to store the node pointer of the entity we want to control:

```
Ogre::SceneNode* _SinbadNode;
```

8. The `FrameListener` instantiation needs this pointer:

```
_listener = new MyFrameListener(window,camera,viewport,_
SinbadNode);
```

9. And the `createScene` function needs to use this pointer to create and store the node of the entity we want to move; modify the code in the function accordingly:

```
_SinbadNode = _sceneManager->getRootSceneNode()-
>createChildSceneNode();
_SinbadNode->attachObject(sinbadEnt);
```

10. Compile and run the application. You should be able to move the entity with the arrow keys:

What just happened?

We added entity movement using the arrow keys in the `FrameListener`. Now our entity floats over the plane like a wizard.

Adding animation

Floating isn't exactly what we wanted; let's add some animation.

Time for action – adding animation

Our model can move but it isn't animated yet, let's change this.

1. The `FrameListener` needs two animation states:

```
Ogre::AnimationState* _aniState;
Ogre::AnimationState* _aniStateTop;
```

2. To get the animation states in the constructor, we need a pointer to the entity:

```
MyFrameListener(Ogre::RenderWindow* win,Ogre::Camera*
cam,Ogre::Viewport* viewport,Ogre::SceneNode* node,Ogre::Entity*
ent)
```

3. With this pointer we can retrieve the `AnimationState` and save them for later use:

```
_aniState = ent->getAnimationState("RunBase");
_aniState->setLoop(false);

_aniStateTop = ent->getAnimationState(«RunTop»);
_aniStateTop->setLoop(false);
```

4. Now that we have the `AnimationState`, we need to have a flag in the `frameStarted` function, which tells us whether or not the entity walked this frame. We add this flag into the `if` conditions that query the keyboard state:

```
bool walked = false;
if(_Keyboard->isKeyDown(OIS::KC_UP))
{
  SinbadTranslate += Ogre::Vector3(0,0,-1);
  _rotation = 3.14f;
  walked = true;
}
if(_Keyboard->isKeyDown(OIS::KC_DOWN))
{
  SinbadTranslate += Ogre::Vector3(0,0,1);
  _rotation = 0.0f;
  walked = true;
}
if(_Keyboard->isKeyDown(OIS::KC_LEFT))
{
  SinbadTranslate += Ogre::Vector3(-1,0,0);
  _rotation = -1.57f;
  walked = true;
}
if(_Keyboard->isKeyDown(OIS::KC_RIGHT))
```

```
{
  SinbadTranslate += Ogre::Vector3(1,0,0);
  _rotation = 1.57f;
  walked = true;
}
```

5. If the model moves, we enable the animation; if the animation has ended, we loop it:

```
if(walked)
{
  _aniState->setEnabled(true);
  _aniStateTop->setEnabled(true);
  if(_aniState->hasEnded())
  {
    _aniState->setTimePosition(0.0f);
  }
  if(_aniStateTop->hasEnded())
  {
    _aniStateTop->setTimePosition(0.0f);
  }
}
```

6. If the model didn't move, we disable the animation and set it to the start position:

```
else
{
  _aniState->setTimePosition(0.0f);
  _aniState->setEnabled(false);
  _aniStateTop->setTimePosition(0.0f);
  _aniStateTop->setEnabled(false);
}
```

7. In each frame, we need to add the passed time to the animation; otherwise, it wouldn't move:

```
_aniState->addTime(evt.timeSinceLastFrame);
_aniStateTop->addTime(evt.timeSinceLastFrame);
```

8. The application now also needs a pointer to the entity:

```
Ogre::Entity* _SinbadEnt;
```

9. We use this pointer while instantiating the FrameListener:

```
_listener = new MyFrameListener(window,camera,viewport,_
SinbadNode,_SinbadEnt);
```

10. And, of course, while creating the entity:

```
_SinbadEnt = _sceneManager->createEntity("Sinbad.mesh");
```

11. Compile and run the application. Now the model should be animated when it moves:

What just happened?

We added animation to our model, which is only enabled when the model is moved.

Have a go hero – looking up what we used

Look up the chapters where we discussed the techniques we used for the last examples.

Summary

We learned a lot in this chapter about creating our own application to start and run Ogre 3D.

Specifically, we covered the following:

- ◆ How the Ogre 3D startup process works
- ◆ How to make our own main loop
- ◆ Writing our own implementation of an application and `FrameListener`

Some topics we have already covered, but this time we combined them to create a more complex application.

We have now learned everything needed to create our own Ogre 3D applications. The next chapter will focus on extending Ogre 3D with other libraries or additional features to make better and prettier applications.

10
Particle Systems and Extending Ogre 3D

This is the last chapter in this book, in which we are going to learn about a topic we haven't touched yet—particle systems. After this, the chapter is going to present some possible extensions and techniques for Ogre 3D, which might be helpful in the future, but aren't needed necessarily for every application.

In this chapter, we will:

- Learn what a particle system is and how it's used
- Create several different particle systems
- Get to know some Ogre 3D extensions
- Be proud that we finished reading this book

So let's get on with it...

Adding a particle system

We are going to attach a smoke particle system to Sinbad, so we will always know where he is hiding.

Time for action – adding a particle system

We are going to use the code from the last example:

1. Create a particle system that uses a predefined particle script. Add the particle system to the same scene node that the Sinbad entity is attached to:

   ```
   Ogre::ParticleSystem* partSystem = _sceneManager->createParticleSy
   stem("Smoke","Examples/Smoke");
   _SinbadNode->attachObject(partSystem);
   ```

2. Compile and run the application. There should be a large amount of smoke coming from Sinbad.

What just happened?

We used an already defined particle script to create a particle system, which we attached to the same node that our entity was attached to. This way, the particle system follows our entity around when it moves.

What is a particle system?

Before we create our own particle system instead of loading a predefined one, we need to discuss what exactly a particle system is. We have seen the effect a particle system creates—in our case, a smoke cone; but how does it create this?

A particle system consists of two to three different constructs—an emitter, a particle, and an affector (optional). The most important of these three is the particle itself, as the name particle system suggests. A particle displays a color or textures using a quad or the point render capability of the graphics cards. When the particle uses a quad, this quad is always rotated to face the camera. Each particle has a set of parameters, including a time to live, direction, and velocity. There are a lot of different parameters, but these three are the most important for the concept of particle systems. The time to live parameter controls the life and death of a particle. Normally, a particle doesn't live for more than a few seconds before it gets destroyed. This effect can be seen in the demo when we look up at the smoke cone. There will be a point where the smoke vanishes. For these particles, the time to live counter reached zero and they got destroyed.

The direction and velocity parameters describe the moving behavior of the particle. In our case, the direction was up.

An emitter creates a predefined number of particles per second and can be seen as the source of the particles. Affectors, on the other hand, don't create particles but change some of their parameters. We haven't seen any affectors in this scene, but we will later. An affector could change the direction, velocity, or color of the particles created by the emitter.

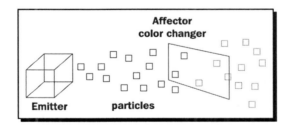

Now that we know the basics, let's create some particle systems on our own.

Creating a simple particle system

To create a particle system, we need to define the behavior of the system at large and the behavior of emitters in particular.

Time for action – creating a particle system

We are going to use the code from the previous example:

1. Particle systems are defined in `.particle` files. Create one in the media/particle folder.

2. Define the system and name it `MySmoke1`:

```
particle_system MySmoke1
{
```

3. Each particle should use the `Example/Smoke` material and be 10 units long and high:

```
material          Examples/Smoke
particle_width    10
particle_height   10
```

4. We want a maximum of 500 particles at the same time and each particle should be a point that always faces the camera:

```
quota             500
billboard_type    point
```

5. We want an emitter that emits the particles from a single point at a rate of 3 particles per second:

```
emitter Point
  {
emission_rate 3
```

6. The particles should be emitted in the direction (1,0,0) with a velocity of 20 units per second:

```
direction 1 0 0
velocity 20
```

7. That's all for this script. Close the brackets:

```
  }
}
```

8. In the `createScene` function, change:

```
Ogre::ParticleSystem* partSystem = _sceneManager->createParticleSy
stem("Smoke","Examples/Smoke");
```

to:

```
Ogre::ParticleSystem* partSystem = _sceneManager->createParticleSy
stem("Smoke","MySmoke1");
```

9. Compile and run the application. You should see Sinbad and a trail of smoke that emerges from him.

What just happened?

We created our first own particle system. For this, we need a `.particle` file to store the script. In this script, we started the definition of the particle system with the keyword `particle_system` and then the name we want it to have, like we did for all the other scripts. In step 3, we defined which material each particle should use. We used a material that ships with the SDK. This material just attaches a texture and combines this texture with the vertex color and ignores any lighting. The following is the complete material script:

```
material Examples/Smoke
{
  technique
  {
    pass
    {
      lighting off
      scene_blend alpha_blend
      depth_write off
      diffuse vertexcolor
      texture_unit
      {
        texture smoke.png
        tex_address_mode clamp
```

```
        }
      }
    }
  }
```

We gave each particle the length and width of 10 units. Step 4 defined the maximum number of particles we want at any given point in the existence of the particle system; this number is helpful in preventing one wrongly defined particle system to slow the complete application down. If this number is reached, no emitter is allowed to create new particles. This step also defined that we want points as particles that always face the camera. Step 5 added an emitter that emits three particles from exactly one point. Step 6 set the direction and speed at which the particles move. We then changed our program to use this new particle system and then saw it in action.

Some more parameters

Now that we have a particle system to experiment with, let's try some other parameters.

Time for action – some new parameters

We will add some new parameter.

1. Add to the point emitter the following three new parameters:

   ```
   angle 30
   time_to_live 10
   color 1 0 0 1
   ```

2. Compile and run the application. You should see red particles flying in slightly different directions.

What just happened?

We added three parameters that changed the behavior of our particle system. Now the particles are red and fly in different directions. The parameter `angle` defines how many degrees each created particle can differentiate from the given direction. Ogre 3D used a random generator to generate the direction, which is in the given range. Because the direction can be moved up to 30 degrees, some of our particles can fly into the ground.

The parameter `time_to_live` sets the lifetime of each particle, in our case, to 10 seconds. The default is 5. And with this, we doubled the life expectations of each particle so we can observe their behavior longer.

The `color` parameter sets the vertex color of the particles to the given color vector, in our case, red.

Pop quiz – what makes a particle system

Name the three components that make a particle system; which of them is optional?

Other parameters

There are a lot of different parameters a particle system can have. Here are some more.

Time for action – time to live and color range

Again we are going to add some parameters to our particle system to see the effect they have.

1. Change `time_to_live` to be a range with a minimum and maximum:

   ```
   time_to_live_min 1
   time_to_live_max 10
   ```

2. Do the same for the color:

   ```
   color_range_start 1 0 0
   color_range_end 0 0 1
   ```

3. Adjust your application code; then compile and run it. You should see different colored particles and some will disappear before others.

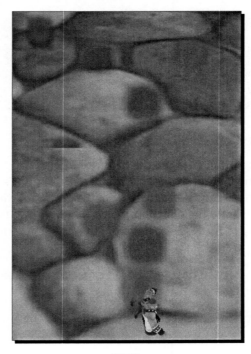

What just happened?

Instead of using single value parameters, we used parameters that described a range of values and let Ogre 3D pick the exact values. This added diversity to our particle system and can be used to model natural effects more realistically, because, in nature, there is seldom something that doesn't have a slightly different appearance over time and space.

Pop quiz – time to live

In your own words, describe the difference between `time_to_live` and `time_to_live_min`.

Turning it on and off again

And even more parameters to try out.

Time for action – adding intervals to a particle system

We will now see that there are also some parameters that don't affect the appearance of the particles, and only affect the way they are emitted.

1. Remove the added parameters of the `point` emitter and only keep the `emission_rate`, `direction`, and `velocity`:

```
emitter Point
{
  emission_rate 30
  direction 1 0 0
  velocity 20
```

2. Then add the parameters that define how long a particle should be emitted and how long to wait before starting over:

```
  duration 1
  repeat_delay 1
}
```

3. Compile and run the application. You should see a stream of white particles, which is briefly interrupted each time the emitter stops emitting.

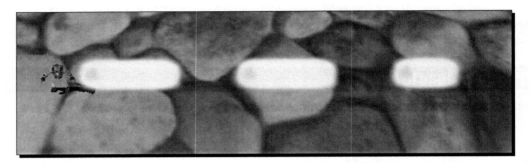

What just happened?

We added the parameter `duration`, which defines how long the emitter will emit particles before ceasing to do so. `repeat_delay` sets the time the emitter will wait before starting to emit particles again. With these two parameters, we have defined an emitter that emits a particle for one second, and then waits for one second and starts over.

Pop quiz – emitter parameters

Try to name all 12 emitter parameters we have used up until now and how they affect the emitter.

Adding affectors

We have changed the behavior and appearance of particles while they were created using the emitter. Now we will use affectors, which change the appearance and behavior during the complete lifetime of a particle.

Time for action – adding a scaler affector

1. To show what an affector does, we need a simple `Point` emitter that emits 30 particles per second with a speed of 20 units and 100 seconds of life:

```
emitter Point
{
  emission_rate 30
  direction 1 0 0
  velocity 20
  time_to_live 100
}
```

2. During the whole lifetime of a particle, we want it to grow five times its size per second. For this, we add a `Scaler` affector:

```
affector Scaler
{
  rate 5
}
```

3. Compile and run the application. You should see particles that get bigger with each second they live.

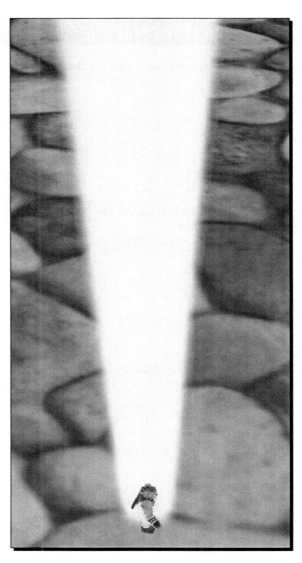

What just happened?

We added an affector that changed the size of our particles for their complete lifetime. The `Scaler` affector scales each particle per second using the given value. In our case, each particle's size was scaled by a factor of five each second.

Changing colors

We have changed the size. Now let's change the color of our particles.

Time for action – changing the color

1. Instead of the scaler, add a `ColorFader` affector that subtracts 0.25 of each color channel per second:

```
affector ColorFader
{
  red -0.25
  green -0.25
  blue -0.25
}
```

2. Compile and run the application. You should see how the white particles get darker with each second they live.

What just happened?

We added an affector that changes each color channel during the existence of a particle, using the predefined values.

Have a go hero – change the color to red

Change the colorfader code so the particles fade from white to red. The result should look like this:

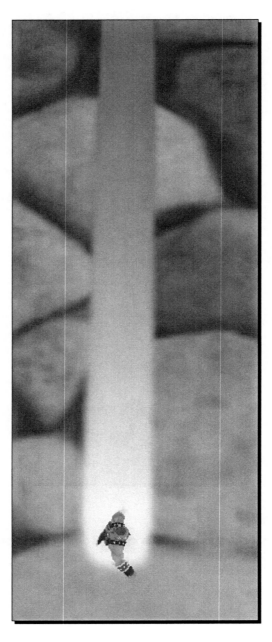

Two-way changing

We have changed one color to another, but sometimes we want the change to depend on the lifetime of the particle. This can be useful when modeling fire or smoke.

Time for action – change depending on the lifetime of a particle

We are now going to introduce more colors by using particle affectors.

1. We don't want our particle to live 100 seconds for this example, so change the lifetime to 4:

```
emitter Point
{
  emission_rate 30
  direction 1 0 0
  velocity 20
  time_to_live 4
}
```

2. Because we want a slightly different behavior, we are going to use the second available colorfader. This should fade each color channel by one unit per second:

```
affector ColorFader2
    {
        red1 -1
        green1 -1
        blue1 -1
```

3. Now, when the particle only has two seconds to live, instead of subtracting the color channel, add the same value we removed beforehand:

```
    state_change 2
    red2 +1
    green2 +1
    blue2 +1
}
```

4. Compile and run the application.

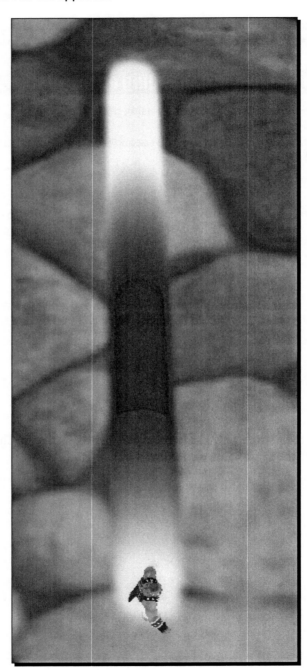

What just happened?

We used the `ColorFader2` affector. This affector first changed each particle with the given values for `red1`, `green1`, and `blue1`, when the particle only had the number of seconds given as the `state_change` parameter to live. Values such as red2, green2, and blue2 were used to modify the particles until they died. In this example, we used this affector to first change the particle from white to black and then when it is two seconds away from dying, we changed the black to white, hence creating the effect seen in the preceding image.

Even more complex color manipulations

There is a way to create even more complex manipulation in regards to the particle color.

Time for action – using complex color manipulation

Once again, we play with particle colors and how we can affect them.

1. We are going to use a new affector called `ColorInterpolator`:

   ```
   affector ColorInterpolator
   {
   ```

2. We then define which color the pixel should have at its creation. We will use white:

   ```
   time0 0
   color0 1 1 1
   ```

3. When the particle has lived for one quarter of its lifetime, it should be red:

   ```
   time1 0.25
   color1 1 0 0
   ```

4. In the second quarter of its lifetime, we want it to be green:

   ```
   time2 0.5
   color2 0 1 0
   ```

5. At three quarters, it should be blue and at the end, white again:

   ```
   time3 0.75
   color3 0 0 1

   time4 1
   color4 1 1 1
   ```

6. Compile and run the application using the new affector, and you should see the stream of particles and they should change from white to red to green to blue and back to white.

What just happened?

We used another affector to create a more complex color manipulation. `ColorInterpolator` manipulated the color of all particles. We defined the manipulation using the keywords **timeX** and **colorX**, where X must be between 0 and 5. `time0 0` means we want the affector to use the color `color0` at the moment the particle is created. `time1 0.25` means we want the affector to use `color1` when the particle has lived one quarter of its lifetime. Between these two points in time the affector interpolates the values. Our example defined five points and each one had a different color. The first and last point used white as the color, the second point used red, the third one green, and the fourth blue. Each point was distanced one quarter of the lifetime apart, so over the complete lifetime, each color was used to the same extent.

Adding randomness

To create a better-looking effect, it can sometimes help to add a bit of randomness to a particle system, so it doesn't look unnatural.

Time for action – adding randomness

Adding randomness can improve the visual quality of a scene, so let's do it.

1. Remove the `ColorInterpolator` affector.

2. Add a different affector called `DirectionRandomiser`:

```
affector DirectionRandomiser
{
```

3. First we define how much influence the affector should have on each axis of our particles:

```
randomness 100
```

4. Then we say how many of our particles should be affected each time the affector is applied. 1.0 stands for 100 percent and 0 for 0 percent. Then we define if we want our particles to keep their velocity or if it should also be changed:

```
scope 1
keep_velocity true
}
```

5. Compile and run the application. This time, you shouldn't see a single stream of particles but, rather, a lot of particles flying in not exactly the same way, but generally in the same direction.

What just happened?

The `DirectionRandomiser` affector changed the direction of our particles, using a different value for each particle. With this affector, it is possible to add a random component to the movement of our particles.

Deflector

The last affector we are going to try out is a plane that deflects particles to simulate an obstacle in their way.

Time for action – using the deflector plane

Being able to let particle bounce of some surface can be helpful, so that is what we are going to do here.

1. Instead of the randomizer, use the `DeflectorPlane` affector:

    ```
    affector DeflectorPlane
    {
    ```

2. The plane is defined using a point in space and the normal of the plane:

    ```
    plane_point 0 20 0
    plane_normal 0 -1 0
    ```

3. The last thing to define is how the plane should affect the particles that hit it. We want them to keep their original velocity, so we select 1.0 as the value:

    ```
      bounce 1.0
    }
    ```

4. To see the effect of the deflector plane, we need our particles to travel in slightly different directions. So modify the emitter such that the particles' directions differ with a maximal value of 30 degrees. Moreover, as the plane hovers in the sky, our particles should have the up vector as the initial direction.

    ```
    emitter Point
    {
      emission_rate 30
      direction 0 1 0
      velocity 20
      time_to_live 4
      angle 30
    }
    ```

5. Compile and run the application. The particles bounce off the invisible plane in the sky.

What just happened?

We added an invisible plane that hovers in the sky and deflects our particles while keeping their velocity.

Have a go hero – doing more with the thing

Create a new application where a second plane at point (0,0,0) deflects the particles that are deflected by the first plane. Also add the `ColorInterpolator` affector. The result should look like the following screenshot:

Other emitter types

We have always used a point emitter for our examples, but, of course, there are different emitter types that we can use.

Time for action – using a box emitter

Only emitting from one point is boring, using a box is much more fun.

1. Change the emitter type from `Point` to `Box`:

```
emitter Box
{
```

2. Define the box in which the particles should be created:

```
height 50
width 50
depth 50
```

3. Let the emitter create 10 particles per second and they should move up with a speed of 20:

```
emission_rate 10
direction 0 1 0
velocity 20
}
```

4. Use the new particle system. Compile and run the application. You should see that particles are created all around the Sinbad instance and fly upwards.

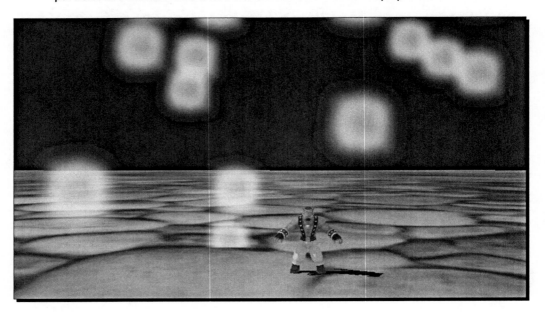

What just happened?

We used another type of emitter, in this case, the `Box` emitter. We defined a box, and the emitter used random points inside this box as the starting position for the created particles. This emitter can be used to create particles systems that don't emit particles from exactly one point, but rather from an area. If we just need a plane where particles are emitted or even a line, we only need to set the box parameters accordingly.

Emitting with a ring

Besides the box, there are other emitter types, like the ring.

Time for action – using a ring to emit particles

Instead of a point or box we can even use a ring as emitter.

1. Change the emitter type to `Ring`:

```
emitter Ring
{
```

2. Define the `Ring` using width and height:

```
height 50
width 50
```

3. Now, to create a ring and not a circle, we need to define how much of the inner part shouldn't emit particles. Here we use percentages:

```
inner_height 0.9
inner_width 0.9
```

4. The rest stays untouched, as follows:

```
    emission_rate 50
    direction 0 1 0
    velocity 20
}
```

5. Compile and run the application. Fly with the camera over the model instance and you should see where the ring emits particles.

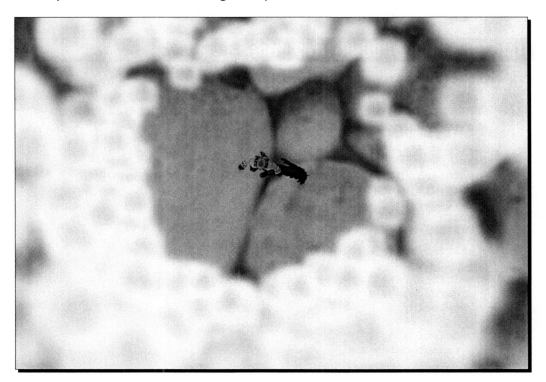

What just happened?

We used the ring emitter to only emit particles in a defined ring. To define the ring, we used height and width, not a point and radius. Width and height describe the largest width and height the circle will have. Here, the following small diagram shows how the circle is defined. With the `inner_width` and `inner_height`, we define how much of the circle's inner area shouldn't emit particles. Here we don't use space units, but percentages.

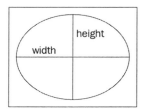

At the end, we would like some fireworks

This will be the last example in this book, so fireworks are appropriate.

Time for action – adding fireworks

It's always nice to see a firework after a special event.

1. Create a particle system that bursts different-colored particles in all directions at a steady interval:

```
particle_system Firework
{
  material           Examples/Smoke
  particle_width     10
  particle_height    10
  quota              5000
  billboard_type     point

  emitter Point
  {
  emission_rate 100
    direction 0 1 0
    velocity 50
    angle 360
    duration 0.1
    repeat_delay 1
    color_range_start 0 0 0
    color_range_end 1 1 1
  }
}
```

2. Create five instances of this particle system:

```
Ogre::ParticleSystem* partSystem1 = _sceneManager->createParticleS
ystem("Firework1","Firework");
Ogre::ParticleSystem* partSystem2 = _sceneManager->createParticleS
ystem("Firework2","Firework");
Ogre::ParticleSystem* partSystem3 = _sceneManager->createParticleS
ystem("Firework3","Firework");
Ogre::ParticleSystem* partSystem4 = _sceneManager->createParticleS
ystem("Firework4","Firework");
Ogre::ParticleSystem* partSystem5 = _sceneManager->createParticleS
ystem("Firework5","Firework");
```

3. Then five nodes at different positions in the sky:

```
Ogre::SceneNode* node1 = _sceneManager->getRootSceneNode()->create
ChildSceneNode(Ogre::Vector3(0,10,0));
Ogre::SceneNode* node2 = _sceneManager->getRootSceneNode()->create
ChildSceneNode(Ogre::Vector3(10,11,0));
Ogre::SceneNode* node3 = _sceneManager->getRootSceneNode()->create
ChildSceneNode(Ogre::Vector3(20,9,0));
Ogre::SceneNode* node4 = _sceneManager->getRootSceneNode()->create
ChildSceneNode(Ogre::Vector3(-10,11,0));
Ogre::SceneNode* node5 = _sceneManager->getRootSceneNode()->create
ChildSceneNode(Ogre::Vector3(-20,19,0));
```

4. Finally, attach the particle systems to their nodes:

```
node1->attachObject(partSystem1);
node2->attachObject(partSystem2);
node3->attachObject(partSystem3);
node4->attachObject(partSystem4);
node5->attachObject(partSystem5);
```

5. Compile and run the application for the last time and enjoy the show

What just happened?

We created a firework-like particle system and duplicated it so it would look like there are several fireworks in the sky.

Pop quiz – different types of emitter

Name all emitter types we have used in this chapter and a few of their differences and similarities.

Extending Ogre 3D

We have seen a lot of different functionalities that Ogre 3D offers, but Ogre 3D also makes it quite easy to extend it with new functions. That's the reason there are a lot of different libraries that can be used to add some new functions to Ogre 3D. We will discuss some of these libraries to get a feeling for what add-ons are out there. A complete list can be found in the wiki at `http://www.Ogre3D.org/tikiwiki/OGRE+Libraries`.

Speedtree

Speedtree is a commercial solution used to render a lot of good-looking trees and grass. It is widely used by several commercial games and the founder of Ogre 3D Sinbad offers a binding for Ogre 3D. Speedtree and the binding for Ogre 3D must be bought and aren't freely available. More information can be found at http://www.ogre3d.org/tikiwiki/ OgreSpeedtree.

Hydrax

Hydrax is an add-on that adds the capability of rendering pretty water scenes to Ogre 3D. With this add-on, water can be added to a scene and a lot of different settings are available, such as setting the depth of the water, adding foam effects, underwater light rays, and so on. The add-on can be found at http://www.ogre3d.org/tikiwiki/Hydrax.

Caelum

Caelum is another add-on, which introduces sky rendering with day and night cycles to Ogre 3D. It renders the sun and moon correctly using a date and time. It also renders weather effects like snow or rain and a complex cloud simulation to make the sky look as real as possible. The wiki site for this add-on is http://www.ogre3d.org/tikiwiki/Caelum.

Particle Universe

Another commercial add-on is **Particle Universe**. Particle Universe adds a new particle system to Ogre 3D, which allows many more different effects than the normal Ogre 3D particle system allows. Also, it comes with a Particle Editor, allowing artists to create particles in a separate application and the programmer can load the created particle script later. This plugin can be found at http://www.ogre3d.org/tikiwiki/ Particle+Universe+plugin.

GUIs

There are a lot of different **GUI** libraries available for Ogre 3D, each of which has its reason to exist, but there isn't one GUI library everyone should use. The best thing is to try out some of them and then decide for ourselves which library suits our needs best.

CEGUI

CEGUI is probably the first GUI library that has been integrated into Ogre 3D. It offers all functions expected from a GUI system and a lot more. There is a GUI editor to create your GUI outside of code and a lot of different skins to customize your GUI. More information can be found at http://www.cegui.org.uk/wiki/index.php/Main_Page.

BetaGUI

BetaGUI is an extremely small library, which comes in one header and one `cpp` file. The only dependency is Ogre 3D and it offers basic functionality like creating windows, buttons, text fields, and static text. It is not a complete GUI, but it offers basic functionality without any dependencies, so it can be used when a simple and quick solution is needed. More can be found at `http://www.ogre3d.org/tikiwiki/BetaGUI`.

QuickGUI

QuickGUI is a more complex and powerful solution than BetaGUI. Though QuickGui offered a lot more widgets, it also made the integration process a bit more difficult. QuickGUI is a full-blown GUI solution that can be used for all kinds of different projects and is updated regularly. The wiki site can be found at `http://www.ogre3d.org/tikiwiki/QuickGUI`.

Berkelium

Berkelium isn't a GUI library as such, as it doesn't have any widgets or anything similar. Instead, it enables Ogre 3D to render websites using the Google Chromium library. With the help of this library, it is possible to build an in-game web browser. The website can be found at `http://www.ogre3d.org/tikiwiki/Berkelium`.

Summary

We learned a lot in this chapter.

Specifically, we covered:

- How to create a particle system using different emitter types
- How affectors can affect particles
- Which add-ons for Ogre 3D are available

The end

This is the end of this book and I would like to congratulate you. I know it is a lot of work to read a complete programming book and do all the examples to understand a new topic, but it is also really rewarding and the new knowledge will be yours forever. I hope you enjoyed this book and it taught you enough to be able to create your own interactive 3D applications, because, in my opinion, this is one of the most interesting and fast-moving areas of programming and computer science in general.

Pop Quiz Answers

Chapter 1

Installing Ogre 3D

1	a	which post effects are shown in the samples	Bloom, Glass, Old TV, Black and White, and Invert
2.1	b and c	which libraries to link	`OgreMain.lib` and `OIS.lib`
2.2		which libraries to link	Add _d after the library name
3	c	`ExampleApplication` and how to display a model	Create an entity using the `createEntity()` function of the `SceneManager` and then attach this entity to a scene node

Chapter 2

Setting up the Environment

1	a	finding the position of scene nodes	MyEntity will be at (60,60,60) and MyEntity2 will be at (0,0,0)
2	b	playing with scene nodes	(10,-10,10)
3	b	rotating a scene node	pitch, yaw, roll
4		creating child scene nodes	4.1)One way is to only give a name for the scene node and the other one is to give a name and a position where the scene node should be created. 4.2) Please refer the code.
5	b	even more about the scene graph	From the root to the leafs
6		Ogre3D and spaces	The three spaces are world, parent, and local.

Chapter 3

Felix Gogo

1	different light sources	A point light is like a light bulb and a spotlight is like a flashlight
2	different light types	Point, Spot, and Directional.

Chapter 4

Felix Gogo

1	c	design pattern of FrameListener	Observer pattern
2		the difference between time- and frame-based movement	When using frame-based movement, the entity is moved the same distance each frame, by time passed movement, the entity is moved the same distance each second.
3		window questions	A window handle is a unique identifier used and created by the operating system to manage its windows, we need the handle of our application window to receive the input events our window gets in focus.
4		capturing the input	To get the newest state the keyboard has

Chapter 5

The Book Inventory Bundle

1	the importance of time	Because this way the animation is independent from the real time that has passed. This also enabled us to run the same animation at different speeds.

Chapter 7

The Bookshelf: First Stab

1	texture modes	How texture coordinates are handled that are lower or higher than the range of 0 to 1

Chapter 9

The Ogre 3D Startup Sequence

1	the three event handlers	`frameStarted` which gets called before the frame is rendered
		`frameRenderingQueued` which is called after the frame is rendered but before the buffers are swapped and
		`frameEnded` which is called after the current frame has been rendered and displayed.

Chapter 10

How About a Graphical Interface?

1	what makes a particle system	Particle, Emitter, and optional Affector
2	emitter parameters	`emission_rate`: How many particles should be emitted per second
		`direction`: In which direction the particles should move
		`velocity`: At which speed they should move
		`duration`: How long does the emitter emit particles
		`repeat_delay`: How long until it start emitting again
		`time_to_live`: The length of the life of a particle
		`time_to_live_min`: The minimum lifespan of a particle
		`time_to_live_max`: The maximum lifespan of a particle
		`angle`: How much the particles' movement direction can differ from the direction given
		`colour`: The color of a particle an particle has
		`colour_range_start`: Beginning point for the particle's color interpolation
		`colour_range_end`: End point for the particle's color interpolation

Index

Symbols

3D model
rendering 50, 51
3D scene
animations, adding 87-90
basic movement control, adding using WASD
keys 77, 78
camera, creating 61, 79, 80
camera, making work 79, 80
creating 67, 68
input support, adding 75, 76
movement, adding 70-72
plane, adding 47
point light, adding 51, 52
second point light, adding 53
shadows, adding 60, 61
spot light, adding 53, 55
swords, adding 97, 98
time-based movement, adding 73
timer, adding 84
two animations, playing at the same
time 91, 92
3D space 21, 22
_keepRunning variable 224

A

addCompositor() function 177
add-ons
list 267, 268
addResourcesLocation() function 109
addTime() function 93
addViewport() function 196

affectors
adding 248
scalar affector, adding 248-250
animated scrolling 146
animation
adding 233-236
animations
about 87, 99
adding, to 3D scene 87-90
printing 100, 101
skeleton, using 99, 100
application class
creating 211-214
attachObjectToBone() function 98

B

basic movement control
adding, to 3D scene 77, 78
begin method 113
Berkelium 268
BetaGUI 268
billboarding 118
blank sheet
creating 103, 104
border color
changing 141, 142
border mode
border color, changing 141, 142
using 140, 141
box emitter
using 261, 262
BSP 109
BspSceneManager
creating 108
build() function 125

C

Caelum 267
camera
  adding 224
  creating 61
capture() function 77
CEGUI 267
child scene nodes
  creating 32
chooseSceneManager() function 108
clamp mode
  using 135-138
color
  changing 250, 251
  changing, particle life time dependent 253, 255
  changing, to red 252
  complex color manipulation 256, 257
color channel
  selecting 198-203
ColorFader2 affector 255
ColorInterpolator 255
ColorInterpolator affector 260
color parameter 245
colorX 257
compositors
  adding 167, 168, 226-229
  combining 173-175
  complex compositors 178-182
  green and blue color channels, swapping 178
  in code, combining 177
  working 169
ConfigFile class 211
configuration file
  structure 211
createCamera() function 61, 194, 196
createChildSceneNode() function 31
createEntity() function 120
createScene() function 19, 47, 97, 100, 130, 168, 186, 194, 202, 230, 233, 243
createScene() method 16
createViewport() function 201
createViewport() method 195
createViewports() function 196
createViewports() method 64
culling 62

D

default_params block 155
deflector plane
  using 259, 260
directional lights
  about 57
  creating 58
DirectionRandomiser 257
DirectionRandomiser affector 258

E

ExampleApplication 15
ExampleApplication class 205

F

falloff parameter 55
field of grass
  creating 118-120
fireworks
  adding 264-266
fixed function pipeline 149
fragment_program keyword 154
fragments 150
frameEnded function 215, 219
  true, returning 219, 220
FrameEvent 74
FrameListener
  about 72
  adding 215, 216, 224, 225
  frameStarted function, true returning in 217
  implementation, experimenting with 216, 217
FrameListener class 216
FrameListener function 217, 218
frameRenderingQueued function
  about 215, 218
  true, returning 218, 219
frameStarted function 215, 216, 218, 221, 227, 234
frameStarted() method 74, 94, 191

G

getAnimationState() function 90
getMouseState() function 81
GUIs 267

grass field
    creating 118-120

H

Hydrax 267

I

image
    inverting 172, 173
initialiseResourceGroup() function 110
input
    adding 220-222
input support
    adding, to 3D scene 75, 76
intervals
    adding, to particle system 247, 248
isKeyDown() function 81

K

keepRunning function 223

L

light
    adding 229-231
loadResources() function 212
local and parent space
    translating in 40
local space 38, 39
lookat() function 62

M

manual object
    about 113
    creating 111
    lines 113
    playing, with 116
    points 113
    triangles 114
material
    another material, creating 133
    creating 131, 132
    inheriting 146-149

mirror mode
    using 138-140
model
    creating, for displaying blades of grass 110, 111
    loading 16
    quad, replacing with 160
models
    loading, resources.cfg used 209, 210
MouseState class 81
movement
    adding, to 3D scene 70-72
moveRelative() function 82
MyVertexShader3 159

N

name scheme
    about 120
    names, printing 120, 121
number of pixels
    changing 182
    changing, while running application 188-193
    putting, in material 183-185

O

Object Oriented Input System(OIS) 14
Octree
    about 106
    diagrammatic representation 106
    example 107, 108
    features 107
OctreeSceneManager 110
Ogre 3D
    downloading 7
    extending 266
    installing 7
    name scheme 120
    starting 205-207
    texture mapping 115
Ogre 3D application
    IDE, configuring 12-14
    project, starting 12-14
Ogre 3D samples
    building 11
Ogre 3D SDK
    downloading 7
    installing 8

versions 8
Ogre scene graph
  about 19, 23, 24
  local space, translating in 40
  RootSceneNode, working with 21
  scene node, creating 19, 20
  scene node position, setting 25-27
  scene node, rotating 26
  scene node, scaling 29
  spaces 35
  spaces, rotating 42
  spaces, scaling 45
  transformation information 35
  tree, building using scene nodes 32, 33
  using 32
oPosition parameter 156
OT_LINE_LIST 113
OT_LINE_STRIP 113
OT_POINT_LIST 113
OT_TRIANGLE_LIST 114
OT_TRIANGLE_STRIP 114
out parameter 155, 156

P

parameters 244, 245
particles
  emitting, ring used 262, 264
particle system
  about 241
  adding 239, 240
  creating 241, 243
  intervals, adding 247, 248
particle universe 267
pitch() function 28, 82
plane
  adding 229-231
  adding, to scene 48
  creating 47, 48
point light
  adding, to scene 51, 52
position() function 114, 122
pulse
  adding 162, 164

Q

quad
  preparing 133, 134
  replacing, with model 160
QuickGUI 268

R

randomness
  adding 257, 258
rendering loop
  using 222, 223
renderOneFrame function 223, 224
render pipeline 150
ResourceGroup 110
ResourceGroupManager 109
resources
  adding 208
resources.cfg
  using, to load models 209, 210
ring
  used, for emitting particles 262, 264
roll() function 28
Root class 206
root instance 208
RootSceneNode
  working with 20, 21

S

scalar affector
  adding 248-250
scale() function 31
scene
  preparing 165, 166
scene graph. *See* **Ogre scene graph**
scene manager
  about 103, 105
  creating 108
  functions 105
  using 108
scene manager's type
  printing 105

scene node
3D space 21
creating, with Ogre3D 19, 20
RootSceneNode, working with 20, 21
rotating 26-28
scaling 29, 31
scene node position
setting 24-27
SDK
exploring 9, 10
setMaterialName() function 148, 149
setPolygonMode() function 84
setPosition() function 30
setShadowTechnique() function 64
setWorldGeometry() function 110
shaders
about 149
shader application 151-155
textures, using 156-158
writing 155
shadows
adding, to scene 60, 61
Sinbad
controlling 77
Sinbad mesh
loading 208, 209
spaces, 3D scene
local space 38, 40
rotating in 42-45
scaling 45
world space 36
Speedtree 267
split screen
adding 193-196
spot light
about 55, 57
adding, to scene 53, 55
light colors, mixing 57
startRendering function 222, 223
startup() function 213, 216, 222, 228
state_change parameter 255
static geometry
about 122
indices 126, 127
pipeline, rendering 125
using 122-124

swords
adding, to 3D scene 97, 98

T

tex2D function 158
texture
modifying 170, 171
scrolling 143-145
textureCoord() function 114, 159
texture count
decreasing 175, 176
texture mapping 115
texture modes
using 142
time-based movement
adding, to 3D scene 73
timer
adding 84
time_to_live
changing 246, 247
timeX 257
translate() function 38
two animations
playing, at the same time in 3D scene 91, 92

U

user control
adding 231
model, controlling with arrow keys 231-233
user input and animation
combining 94-96

V

variable
in code, setting 185
setting, from application 185-187
vertex 113
viewport
about 64, 197
creating 64, 65
volume
adding, to blades of grass 116, 117

W

white quad
  creating 130, 131
window handle 76, 77
wireframe and point render mode
  adding, to framelistener 82-84
world space
  translating in 36, 37
wrapping mode
  using, with another texture 135, 137

Y

yaw() function 28, 82
y-up convention 22

Thank you for buying
Ogre 3D 1.7 Beginner's Guide

About Packt Publishing

Packt, pronounced 'packed', published its first book "*Mastering phpMyAdmin for Effective MySQL Management*" in April 2004 and subsequently continued to specialize in publishing highly focused books on specific technologies and solutions.

Our books and publications share the experiences of your fellow IT professionals in adapting and customizing today's systems, applications, and frameworks. Our solution based books give you the knowledge and power to customize the software and technologies you're using to get the job done. Packt books are more specific and less general than the IT books you have seen in the past. Our unique business model allows us to bring you more focused information, giving you more of what you need to know, and less of what you don't.

Packt is a modern, yet unique publishing company, which focuses on producing quality, cutting-edge books for communities of developers, administrators, and newbies alike. For more information, please visit our website: www.packtpub.com.

About Packt Open Source

In 2010, Packt launched two new brands, Packt Open Source and Packt Enterprise, in order to continue its focus on specialization. This book is part of the Packt Open Source brand, home to books published on software built around Open Source licences, and offering information to anybody from advanced developers to budding web designers. The Open Source brand also runs Packt's Open Source Royalty Scheme, by which Packt gives a royalty to each Open Source project about whose software a book is sold.

Writing for Packt

We welcome all inquiries from people who are interested in authoring. Book proposals should be sent to author@packtpub.com. If your book idea is still at an early stage and you would like to discuss it first before writing a formal book proposal, contact us; one of our commissioning editors will get in touch with you.

We're not just looking for published authors; if you have strong technical skills but no writing experience, our experienced editors can help you develop a writing career, or simply get some additional reward for your expertise.

Unity Game Development Essentials

ISBN: 978-1-847198-18-1   Paperback: 316 pages

Build fully functional, professional 3D games with realistic environments, sound, dynamic effects, and more!

1. Kick start game development, and build ready-to-play 3D games with ease

2. Understand key concepts in game design including scripting, physics, instantiation, particle effects, and more

3. Test & optimize your game to perfection with essential tips-and-tricks

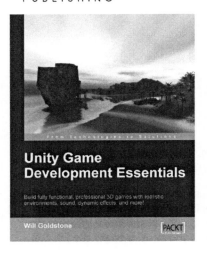

3D Game Development with Microsoft Silverlight 3: Beginner's Guide

ISBN: 978-1-847198-92-1   Paperback: 452 pages

A practical guide to creating real-time responsive online 3D games in Silverlight 3 using C#, XBAP WPF, XAML, Balder, and Farseer Physics Engine

1. Develop online interactive 3D games and scenes in Microsoft Silverlight 3 and XBAP WPF

2. Integrate Balder 3D engine 1.0, Farseer Physics Engine 2.1, and advanced object-oriented techniques to simplify the game development process

Please check **www.PacktPub.com** for information on our titles

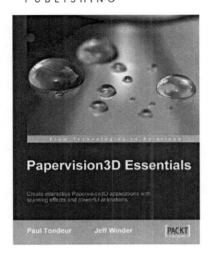

Papervision3D Essentials

ISBN: 978-1-847195-72-2   Paperback: 428 pages

Create interactive Papervision 3D applications with stunning effects and powerful animations

1. Build stunning, interactive Papervision3D applications from scratch

2. Export and import 3D models from Autodesk 3ds Max, SketchUp and Blender to Papervision3D

3. In-depth coverage of important 3D concepts with demo applications, screenshots and example code.

Blender 3D 2.49 Incredible Machines

ISBN: 978-1-847197-46-7   Paperback: 316 pages

Modeling, rendering, and animating realistic machines with Blender 3D

1. Walk through the complete process of building amazing machines

2. Model and create mechanical models and vehicles with detailed designs

3. Add advanced global illumination options to the renders created in Blender 3D using YafaRay and LuxRender

Please check **www.PacktPub.com** for information on our titles

Lightning Source UK Ltd.
Milton Keynes UK
UKOW020732290413

209923UK00002B/19/P